THE CONTENTS

OF THE

FIFTH AND SIXTH BOOKS
OF EUCLID

(WITH A NOTE ON IRRATIONAL NUMBERS)

THE CONTENTS

OF THE

FIFTH AND SIXTH BOOKS
OF EUCLID

(WITH A NOTE ON IRRATIONAL NUMBERS)

ARRANGED AND EXPLAINED

BY

M. J. M. HILL, M.A., D.Sc., F.R.S.

ASTOR PROFESSOR OF MATHEMATICS IN THE UNIVERSITY OF LONDON
LATE EXAMINER IN THE UNIVERSITY OF LONDON
AND FOR THE CIVIL SERVICE OF INDIA

SECOND EDITION

CAMBRIDGE:
AT THE UNIVERSITY PRESS
1908

CAMBRIDGE
UNIVERSITY PRESS

University Printing House, Cambridge CB2 8BS, United Kingdom

Published in the United States of America by Cambridge University Press, New York

Cambridge University Press is part of the University of Cambridge.

It furthers the University's mission by disseminating knowledge in the pursuit of education, learning and research at the highest international levels of excellence.

www.cambridge.org
Information on this title: www.cambridge.org/9781107415898

© Cambridge University Press 1908

First edition 1900
Second edition 1908
First published 1908
First paperback edition 2014

A catalogue record for this publication is available from the British Library

ISBN 978-1-107-41589-8 Paperback

*PREFACE TO THE SECOND EDITION.

THE object of this work is to remove the chief difficulties felt by those who desire to understand the Sixth Book of Euclid. With the exception of the note at the end of the book on irrational numbers, which is intended for teachers and advanced students only, it contains nothing beyond the capacity of those who have mastered the first four Books, and has been prepared for their use. It is the result of an experience of teaching the subject extending over more than twenty years.

The Sixth Book depends to a very large extent on the Fifth, but this Fifth Book is so difficult that in actual teaching it is usually entirely omitted with the exception of the Fifth Definition, which is retained not for the purpose of proving all the properties of ratio required in the Sixth Book, but only for demonstrating two important propositions, viz., the 1st and 33rd.

The other properties of ratio required in the Sixth Book are usually assumed, or so-called algebraic demonstrations are supplied. The employment side by side of these two methods of dealing with ratio confuses the learner, because, not being equivalent, they do not constitute, when used in this way, a firm basis for the train of reasoning which he is attempting to follow. A better method is sometimes attempted. This is to insist on the mastering of the Fifth Book, expressed in modern form as in the Syllabus of the Association for the Improvement of Geometrical Teaching, before commencing the Sixth Book.

But it is far too difficult for all but the best pupils, and even they do not grasp the train of reasoning as a whole, though they readily admit the truth of the propositions singly as consequences of the fundamental definitions, which are

(I)   The fifth definition, which is the test for the sameness of two ratios.

(II)   The seventh definition, which is the test for distinguishing the greater of two unequal ratios from the smaller.

* The alterations which have been introduced into this second edition are so extensive that the preface to the first edition would not be intelligible without a copy of the text. That preface has therefore not been reprinted. So much of it as is relevant to the second edition is here incorporated.

*(III)   The tenth definition, which defines "Duplicate Ratio."

*(IV)   The definition marked A by Simson, which defines the process for compounding ratios.

In order to make things clear, it is necessary to explain what it is that makes Euclid's Fifth Book so very difficult.

There is first the difficulty arising out of Euclid's notation for magnitudes and numbers. This has been entirely removed in most modern editions by using an algebraic notation and need not therefore be further considered.

There is next the difficulty arising out of Euclid's use of the word "ratio," and the idea represented by it.

His definition of ratio (see Note 4) furnishes no satisfactory answer to the question, "What is a ratio?" and it is of such a nature that no indication is afforded of the answer to the still more important question, "How is a ratio to be measured?" As Euclid makes no use of the definition in his argument, it is useless to examine it further, but it is worth while to try to get at his view of ratio. He asserts indirectly that a ratio is a magnitude, because in the seventh definition he states the conditions which must be satisfied in order that one ratio may be *greater* than another. Now the word "greater" can only be applied to a magnitude. Hence Euclid must have considered a ratio to be a magnitude†. To this conclusion it may be objected that if Euclid thought that a ratio was a magnitude he would not so constantly have spoken of the *sameness* of two ratios, but of their *equality*. One can only surmise that, whenever it was possible, he desired to leave open all questions as to the nature of ratio, and to present all his propositions as logical deductions from his fundamental definitions. Yet the question as to the nature of ratio is one which forces itself on the careful reader, and is a source of the greatest perplexity, culminating when he reaches the 11th and 13th Propositions.

The 11th Proposition may be stated thus:—

If	$A : B$ is the same as $C : D$,
and if	$C : D$ is the same as $E : F$,
then	$A : B$ is the same as $E : F$.

Now if a ratio is a magnitude, this only expresses that if $X = Y$, and if $Y = Z$, then $X = Z$.

As this result follows from Euclid's First Axiom it is difficult to see the need for a proof.

---

* These are not required until the 6th Book is reached.

† Some writers maintain that the word "greater" as applied to ratio, is not used in the same sense as when it is applied to magnitudes. This seems to make matters far more difficult.

This only becomes apparent when the reader realises that Euclid's procedure may be described thus:—

Let A, B, C, D be four magnitudes satisfying the conditions of the Fifth Definition, and let C, D, E, F be four magnitudes also satisfying the same conditions, then it is to be proved that A, B, E, F also satisfy the conditions of that definition (see Art. 175).

Remarks of a somewhat similar nature apply to the 13th Proposition.

The next difficulty to be considered is the indirectness of Euclid's line of argument, arising from the fact that he uses the Seventh Definition where the Fifth alone need be employed. His Fifth Definition states the conditions which must be satisfied in order that two ratios may be the same (or if ratios are magnitudes, that they may be equal).

If this definition is a good and sound one, it is evident that it ought to be possible to deduce from it all the properties of equal ratios. This is in fact the case. It is wholly unnecessary to employ the Seventh Definition, which refers to unequal ratios, to prove any of the properties of equal ratios. Its use only renders the proofs of the Propositions indirect and artificial and consequently difficult. Not only does no inconvenience result from avoiding its use, but it is possible to get rid of the latter part of the 8th Proposition, and of the whole of the 10th and 13th Propositions, which deal with unequal ratios, and of the 14th, 20th and 21st Propositions of the Fifth Book, which are particular cases of the 16th, 22nd and 23rd Propositions respectively.

The remaining Propositions are demonstrated by means of the Fifth Definition alone; and all, with three exceptions, fall under one or other of two well recognized types, which correspond to the two forms of the conditions for the equality of two ratios (Arts. 46, 48).

The first form of the conditions is Euclid's Test for Equal Ratios as stated in the Fifth Definition of the Fifth Book. It contains three classes of alternatives, one of which appears only when the magnitudes of the ratios are commensurable. Sometimes it is possible to examine all three classes of alternatives in the same way. On the other hand, in the extremely important Propositions Euc. V. 16, 22, 23, the examination of the cases in which the ratios are commensurable has to be conducted upon different lines to those which are applicable when they are not commensurable. This it is quite possible to do, but the line of argument is artificial and therefore difficult for a beginner, as will be seen by consulting Notes 6, 9 and 11 at the end of the book. The proofs of Euc. V. 16, 22, 23 as completed by these Notes depend on the use of Prop. 63 (Euc. V. 4), but the way in which that proposition has to be used does not suggest itself naturally.

It is on this account that the second form of the conditions for the equality of two ratios (Art. 48) has been introduced into this book. So far as the Author knows it was first published by Stolz (see Arts. 47, 48).

Reference has been made above to three Propositions which do not fall under either of the above recognized types. These are Prop. 62 (Euc. V. 24), Prop. 65 (Euc. V. 19), Prop. 66 (Euc. V. 25). The proofs here given are Euclid's. They are very much shorter than any direct deduction of the propositions from either form of the conditions for the equality of two ratios. At the same time their artificial character stands out in striking contrast to the directness of the proofs of the other propositions.

A still greater difficulty than any of the preceding arises from the fact that Euclid furnishes no explanation of the steps by which he reached his fundamental definitions.

To write down a definition, and then draw conclusions from it, is a process which is useful in Advanced Mathematics; but it is wholly unsuitable for elementary teaching. It seems not unlikely that Euclid reached his fundamental definitions as conclusions to elaborate trains of reasoning, but that finding great difficulty in expressing this reasoning in words owing to the absence of an algebraic notation, he preferred to write down his definitions as the basis of his argument, and to present the propositions as logical deductions from his definitions.

Apparently he has left no trace of the steps by which he reached his fundamental definitions; and one of the chief objects of this book is to reconstruct a path which can be followed by beginners from ideas of a simpler order to those on which his work is based.

The most important of his definitions is the Fifth, on reaching which the beginner, who has read the first four books of Euclid, experiences a sense of discontinuity. He knows nothing which can lead him directly to it, he has no ideas of a simpler order with which to connect it; and he is therefore reduced to learning it by rote. His teacher may show him that it contains the definition of Proportion given in treatises on Algebra; but even with this assistance it remains difficult for him to remember its details. He may and frequently does learn to apply it correctly in demonstrating the 1st and 33rd Propositions of the Sixth Book, but the Author's experience both of teaching and examining leads him to the belief that it is not really understood.

In the first edition of this book, the writer, following a suggestion due to the late Professor De Morgan, derived Euclid's Test for the Sameness (or Equality) of Two Ratios from the Theory of Relative Multiple Scales, and on this theory the whole treatment of the subject was based. This procedure made it possible to render Euclid's Fifth Book intelligible even to persons not possessed of any special mathematical aptitude, but further study of the subject has led the writer to the conclusion that ideas of a still simpler nature may be taken as a starting point, and accordingly the use of the above-mentioned theory has been replaced by a direct comparison of ratios with rational fractions.

The arrangement of the argument may be briefly summarised thus:—

The first thing to be done is to consider the ideas connected with the term magnitude. No attempt is made to define a magnitude*; all that is done is to enumerate the characteristic properties of a magnitude.

It is easy to give illustrations of what is meant by a magnitude, such as a segment of a straight line, an area, a volume, or a weight. In regard to these it is assumed that if any magnitude, which may be called A, exists, then any number of magnitudes exist having exactly the same properties. Each of these is called A, and it is assumed to be possible to add any number of them together to form a new magnitude. Thus if r denote any integer, and r magnitudes each equal to A are added together, the sum is called rA.

Conversely if any magnitude B exist it is assumed that another magnitude A exists, such that $B = rA$. It should be carefully noticed that nothing more than the existence of A is assumed. It is not assumed that it is possible to construct the magnitude A when B is given.

The next step taken is to state the characteristic property of "magnitudes of the same kind." It is easy to give illustrations of what is meant by such magnitudes, e.g. two segments of straight lines, or two areas, or two volumes, or two weights, and so on.

But in order to employ such magnitudes in analysis, something further is required. This is expressed as follows:—

Any two magnitudes are said to be of the same kind, whenever it is possible to determine whether any multiple whatever that may be selected of one magnitude is greater than, equal to, or less than any multiple whatever of the other magnitude (Art. 21). In the next place the Axiom of Archimedes is assumed to hold good for any two magnitudes of the same kind (Art. 22). Then the ratio of two commensurable magnitudes is defined in the usual way, viz.:—

The ratio of rA to sA, where r, s denote any two positive integers, is defined to be the rational fraction $\dfrac{r}{s}$ (Art. 30).

---

* It is not now usual to attempt to define a straight line. All that is done is to state the characteristic property of the straight line that it is determined by two points.

It is then proved (Art. 42) that if three magnitudes A, B, C have a common measure,

and if $\qquad\qquad A = B$, then $A : C = B : C$;

but if $\qquad\qquad A > B$, then $A : C .> B : C$.

These are the earlier parts of Propositions 7 and 8 of Euclid's Fifth Book, but up to this stage in the argument they have been proved only if the magnitudes concerned are commensurable.

If two magnitudes have no common measure, then the definition given for the ratio of commensurable magnitudes does not apply, and the definition of ratio must be extended before it can be applied to incommensurable magnitudes. This requires for its full explanation the introduction into the subject of the irrational number. As this is too difficult for the majority of those for whom this book is written, it is given in a note* at the end of the book, whilst in the text it is simply stated that the irrational number is a "magnitude† of the same kind" (in the sense explained above) as the rational fraction, and a method of arranging all ratios, whether they be ratios of commensurable or incommensurable magnitudes, in order of magnitude, is constructed on the hypothesis that the propositions :—

If $\qquad\qquad A = B$, then $A : C = B : C$,

and if $\qquad\qquad A > B$, then $A : C > B : C$

hold good, whenever the magnitudes A, B, C are of the same kind in the sense explained above, whether they have or have not a common measure (Art. 43).

When irrational numbers have been defined, it is shown that if A, B be magnitudes of the same kind which are incommensurable, then the ratio of A to B is an irrational number. (Arts. 208—210.)

The hypotheses stated in the last paragraph but one make it possible to compare any ratio with any rational fraction, and to determine whether any two ratios are equal or unequal, and if unequal which is the greater. Thus Euclid's Tests, given in his Fifth and Seventh Definitions, are obtained.

Euclid however deduces the Propositions just mentioned, which have been taken as hypotheses, from his Fifth and Seventh Definitions. These two definitions present very great difficulties to the beginner. Their meaning is far more difficult to grasp than the propositions quoted above. Accordingly in this second edition the order of the argument has been inverted.

* Note 15.

† In the purely arithmetical theory a number is primarily a mark of order, and not a magnitude. This purely arithmetical conception of a number if insisted upon in the text would have made the argument of too abstract a nature to be readily understood by those for whose use it is written.

This is the principal change made in the argument. But it is of so far-reaching a character that it has rendered it necessary to re-write the greater part of the book.

This method of treatment leads naturally to Dedekind's Theory of the Irrational Number, which, as already mentioned, is explained in a note* at the end of the book, the material of which is drawn largely from Dedekind's work.

In this edition a section is devoted to the consideration of the ratios of Commensurable Magnitudes, with the object of making it easier to understand the treatment of the ratios of incommensurable magnitudes which follows.

The technical terms "Compounding of Ratios" and "Duplicate Ratio" present some difficulty to beginners. So far as the Sixth Book of Euclid is concerned, they are only required for the construction of two straight lines whose ratio is equal to the ratio of two areas. The constructions present no difficulty and are given in the text (Art. 36, Props. 40 and 42), whilst the technical terms are relegated to notes in the Appendix (see Notes 13, 14). The effect of these constructions is to reduce the measurement of areas to the measurement of lengths.

Several alterations have been made in the order of the Propositions. De Morgan pointed out that learners found great difficulty in reading the Fifth Book on account of the abstract character of the reasoning, its application to something concrete not being easily perceived. Accordingly in this work Propositions from the Sixth Book are taken as soon as a sufficient number of Propositions from the Fifth Book have been proved to make it possible to deal logically with those in the Sixth Book. With regard to the enunciations no attempt has been made to adhere to Euclid's words.

This work contains demonstrations of all† the Propositions in the Fifth Book except Nos. 8, 10, 13 which depend on the Seventh Definition, and which are not required for the understanding of the Sixth Book.

It contains also the demonstrations of all the Propositions in the Sixth Book except No. 32, which is of no importance.

---

* It is hoped that what is there set down will induce some of my readers to study Dedekind's own Tract on Continuity and Irrational Numbers. There is an English Translation by Professor Beman, published by the Open Court Publishing Company, of which the London Agents are Kegan Paul, Trench, Trübner & Co.

† The demonstration of Euc. V. 3 is involved in the proof of the Proposition here numbered 5. Euc. V. 20 is a particular case of Euc. V. 22, here numbered 37. Euc. V. 21 is a particular case of Euc. V. 23, here numbered 57.

The Propositions here numbered 7, 8, 13, 14, 26, 39, 60, 61, 64 and 69 are not in Euclid's Text.

There are given in suitable positions in the book, the definitions of Harmonic Points and Lines, of the Pole and Polar, of Inversion, of the Radical Axis and the Centres of Similitude of Two Circles, and (so far as is possible without explaining the use of the Negative Sign in Geometry) of Cross or Anharmonic Ratio, with the sole object of rendering intelligible the terminology employed in a number of interesting examples in the book.

The harder examples are marked with an asterisk.

The Author believes that he has not taken without acknowledgment from other text-books anything which is not common property.

His special thanks are due to the Cambridge University Press Syndicate, who have made the publication of the book possible; and to his friend and former pupil, Dr L. N. G. Filon, for valuable suggestions and assistance.

He will be grateful to his readers for suggestions and corrections.

TABLE OF CONTENTS.

SECTION I.

SECTION II.

SECTION III.

Propositions 13, 14.   On Ratio.

SECTION IV.

SECTION V.

Propositions 27—34. Similar Figures.

SECTION IX.

PROPOSITIONS 51—56. MISCELLANEOUS GEOMETRICAL PROPOSITIONS.

SECTION X.

SECTION XI.

ERRATUM.

Page 152, line 22.   *For* 'segments of straight lines' *read* 'magnitudes of the same kind.'

LIST OF ABBREVIATIONS.

$+$	Plus.
$-$	Minus.
$=$	Equal to.
$<$	Less than.
$>$	Greater than.
$\neq$	Not equal to.
$\not<$	Not less than.
$\not>$	Not greater than.
$A \sim B$	The difference of A and B.
$A : B$	The ratio of A to B.
$A : B = C : D$	The ratio of A to B is equal to the ratio of C to D.
$*$	Compounded with. (Art. 191.)
$\frown$	Aggregated with. (Art. 194.)

SECTION I.

PROPOSITIONS 1—8.
ON MAGNITUDES, THEIR MULTIPLES AND THEIR MEASURES.

Art. 1. Number.

IN this book except where otherwise stated the word Number will be used as an abbreviation for Positive Whole Number.

Notation for Number.

A Number will always be denoted by a *small* letter.

Art. 2. Notation for Magnitude.

A Magnitude will be denoted throughout this book by a *capital* letter*.

Art. 3. *Def.* 1. MULTIPLE.

If A denote any magnitude, then it is usual to denote $A + A$ by $2A$ for brevity, and in like manner $A + A + A$ by $3A$ for brevity and so on. If A be added successively to itself until there are in the aggregate altogether r A's, the result is written rA for brevity, and called the rth multiple of A.

It follows from the definition that

$$rA + A = (r+1) A.$$

If the magnitude B be the same as rA, then B is said to be a multiple of A, and in general

One magnitude is said to be a multiple of another magnitude, when the former contains the latter an exact number of times.

It will be in agreement with the above nomenclature, when A is equal to B, to say that A is the first multiple of B; and to call the rth multiple of B and the rth multiple of C the *same* multiples of B and C.

---

* A point will also be denoted by a capital letter, but this will not lead to any difficulty.

Art. 4. It is necessary to prove certain propositions regarding magnitudes and multiples of magnitudes before entering upon the discussion of the relations between magnitudes.

These propositions depend upon the Commutative and Associative Laws for Addition.

The Commutative Law is expressed by the formula

$$X + Y = Y + X.$$

The Associative Law is expressed by the formula

$$(X + Y) + Z = X + (Y + Z).$$

The effect of these two laws is to render it permissible, when adding up any number of magnitudes, to group them in any way, to add up the members of each group, and then to add up the groups.

Art. 5.   PROPOSITION I.*   (Euc. V. 1.)

ENUNCIATION.   *To prove that* $r(A + B) = rA + rB.$

Since $\quad\quad\quad\quad rA$ means $A + A + A + \ldots$ to r terms,

$\quad r(A + B)$ means $(A + B) + (A + B) + (A + B) + \ldots$ to r terms.

By means of the commutative and associative laws, the terms in the r groups may be added up in any order.

Adding up the r A's together, the result is rA, and adding up the r B's together the result is rB.

Thus $\quad\quad\quad\quad\quad\quad r(A + B) = rA + rB.$

Art. 6.   EXAMPLE 1.

By repeated application of Proposition I. prove that

$$r(A + B + \ldots + K) = rA + rB + \ldots + rK.$$

Art. 7.   PROPOSITION II.*   (Euc. V. 2.)

ENUNCIATION.   *To prove that* $(a + b) R = aR + bR.$

By definition $(a + b) R$ means $R + R + \ldots$ until there are $(a + b)$ terms.

By the Associative Law these terms may be added up in any way.

---

* A more formal proof of this theorem will be found in the Appendix, see Note 2.

Take therefore the first a R's and put them in one group, and put the remaining b R's into another group.

The sum of the first group is aR.

The sum of the second group is bR.

$$\therefore \ (a + b) R = aR + bR.$$

Art. 8. EXAMPLES.

2. Prove that $(r + s + t + \dots + z) A = rA + sA + tA + \dots + zA.$

3. If A and B are both multiples of G, prove that $A + B$ is a multiple of G.

Art. 9. PROPOSITION III.* (Euc. V. 5.)

ENUNCIATION. *If $A > B$, then $r (A - B) = rA - rB$.*

Since $A > B,$

let $A = B + C.$

$$\therefore \ rA = r (B + C)$$
$$= rB + rC. \qquad\qquad \text{[Prop. 1.}$$
$$\therefore \ rC = rA - rB.$$

But $C = A - B,$

$$\therefore \ r (A - B) = rA - rB.$$

Art. 10. PROPOSITION IV.* (Euc. V. 6.)

ENUNCIATION. *If $a > b$, prove that $(a - b) R = aR - bR$.*

Since $a > b$, and each is a positive integer,

$\therefore \ (a - b)$ is a positive integer which may be called c.

$$\therefore \ a = b + c.$$
$$\therefore \ aR = (b + c) R$$
$$= bR + cR. \qquad\qquad \text{[Prop. 2.}$$
$$\therefore \ cR = aR - bR.$$
$$\therefore \ (a - b) R = aR - bR.$$

* See Note 1.

Art. 11. EXAMPLE 4.

If A and B are multiples of G, then the difference of A and B is a multiple of G.

Art. 12. PROPOSITION V.*

ENUNCIATION. *To prove that*

$$r(sA) = rs(A) = sr(A) = s(rA).$$

Let a rectangle be drawn and divided into compartments standing in r columns and s rows.

Place the magnitude A in each compartment.

Then the sum of the magnitudes in any row is rA, and the sum of those in any column is sA.

Since there are s rows, the sum of all the magnitudes is $s(rA)$.

Since there are r columns, the sum of all the magnitudes is $r(sA)$.

If the number of the magnitudes be counted, it is rs, or it may also be expressed as sr.

Hence the sum can be written in either of the forms $rs(A)$ or $sr(A)$.

But by the Commutative and Associative Laws the sum of the magnitudes is the same in whatever way the magnitudes are added together.

$$\therefore\ r(sA) = rs(A) = sr(A) = s(rA).$$

Art. 13. EXAMPLE 5.

If A and B are multiples of G, then the sum and difference of rA and sB are multiples of G.

Art. 14. PROPOSITION VI (i).

ENUNCIATION. *If $A > B$, then $rA > rB$;*

If $A = B$, then $rA = rB$;

If $A < B$, then $rA < rB$.

If $A > B,$

let $A = B + C.$

* See Note 1.

$$\therefore \ rA = r(B + C)$$
$$= rB + rC. \qquad \text{[Prop. 1.}$$
$$\therefore \ rA > rB.$$

If $A = B,$

then $rA = rB.$

If $A < B,$

then $B > A.$

Hence $rB > rA,$ by what is proved above.

$$\therefore \ rA < rB.$$

Art. 15.   PROPOSITION VI (ii).

ENUNCIATION.   *If $rA > rB$, then $A > B$;*

If $rA = rB$, then $A = B$;

If $rA < rB$, then $A < B$.

If $rA > rB,$

suppose if possible that A is not greater than B.

Then either $A = B,$

or $A < B.$

But by the first part of this proposition,

if $A = B,$ then $rA = rB$;

and if $A < B,$ then $rA < rB.$

Both these results are contradictory to the hypothesis that $rA > rB$.

Hence A must be greater than B.

The second and third cases can be proved in like manner.

Art. 16.   PROPOSITION VI (iii).

ENUNCIATION.   *If $a > b$, then $aR > bR$;*

If $a = b$, then $aR = bR$;

If $a < b$, then $aR < bR$.

If $a > b,$

let $a = b + c,$

$$\therefore\ aR = (b + c)\,R$$
$$= bR + cR; \quad\quad\quad \text{[Prop. 2.}$$
$$\therefore\ aR > bR.$$

If
$$a = b,$$
then
$$aR = bR.$$
If
$$a < b,$$
then
$$b > a,$$
$$\therefore\ bR > aR, \text{ by what was proved above.}$$
$$\therefore\ aR < bR.$$

Art. 17.   PROPOSITION VI (iv).

ENUNCIATION.   *If $aR > bR$, then $a > b$;*
If $aR = bR$, then $a = b$;
If $aR < bR$, then $a < b$.

If
$$aR > bR,$$
suppose if possible that a is not greater than b.

Then either
$$a = b,$$
or
$$a < b.$$

But by part (iii) of this proposition,

            if $a = b$, then $aR = bR$;

and   if $a < b$, then $aR < bR$.

Both these results are contradictory to the hypothesis that
$$aR > bR.$$

Hence a must be greater than b.

The second and third cases can be proved in like manner.

Art. 18.   EXAMPLES.

6.   (i)   If
$$aU > bV,$$
$$bT > cU,$$
prove that
$$aT > cV.$$
      (ii)   If
$$nrU > tV,$$
and
$$tT > nsU,$$
prove that
$$rT > sV.$$

7.* If $\qquad\qquad rA > sB,$

and $\qquad\qquad\qquad\qquad rC < sD,$

prove that no integers r', s' can exist such that

$$r'A < s'B,$$

and $\qquad\qquad\qquad\qquad r'C > s'D.$

Art. 19. If $B = rA$, then B was called the rth multiple of A.

The magnitude B is said to be measured by A; and A is called a measure or a part† of B.

When A exists, it is assumed to be always possible to *construct* a magnitude equal to rA.

But the reverse operation is not always possible.

When B is a segment of a straight line, a construction can be given, see Prop. 10, for finding the segment of a straight line A, such that $B = rA$.

But if B is an arc of a circle, there exists no known general construction for an arc A, such that $B = rA$ for all values of the integer r.

Nevertheless it will be assumed that if B be any magnitude, and r any positive integer, then a magnitude A exists, whether it can be constructed or not, such that

$$B = rA.$$

This same relation between A and B is denoted by

$$A = \frac{B}{r},$$

or

$$A = \frac{1}{r} B.$$

Art. 20. PROPOSITION VII.

ENUNCIATION. *If the magnitudes A and rA be each divided into s equal parts, prove that any one of the parts into which rA is divided will be r times as great as any one of the parts into which A is divided.*

Suppose that each of the parts into which A is divided is B.

Then $\qquad\qquad\qquad\qquad A = sB.$

$$\therefore rA = rsB = s(rB). \qquad\qquad\text{[Prop. 5.}$$

Hence each of the s equal parts into which rA is divided is rB, which is r times as great as each of the s equal parts into which A is divided.

† The word part is here used in a technical sense. It does not mean any portion of B.

If then $\dfrac{A}{s}$ denote the sth part of A,

$\dfrac{rA}{s}$ will denote the sth part of rA,

and this proposition may be expressed thus:—

$$\frac{rA}{s} = rB = r\left(\frac{A}{s}\right).$$

$$\therefore \frac{rA}{s} = r\left(\frac{A}{s}\right).$$

Art. 21. MAGNITUDES OF THE SAME KIND.

It is usual to speak of two lengths as magnitudes of the same kind, or two areas, or two volumes, or two weights.

The characteristic of two such magnitudes is this:—

It is supposed to be possible always to find out whether any multiple of the one is greater than, or is equal to, or is less than any multiple of the other.

Let the magnitudes be A and B.

Take any multiple of A say rA, and any multiple of B say sB.

Then all that is meant by saying that A and B are of the same kind is this:—

It is assumed to be possible always to determine whether rA is greater than sB, or equal to sB, or less than sB.

In particular it is assumed to be possible to determine whether A is greater than B, or equal to B, or less than B.

The same thing may be put in a slightly different way thus:—

Suppose that B is divided into r equal parts, each of which is denoted by $\dfrac{B}{r}$; that s of these parts are taken, giving $s\left(\dfrac{B}{r}\right)$, then it is supposed to be possible always to determine whether A is greater than, equal to, or less than $s\left(\dfrac{B}{r}\right)$.

If
$$A > s\left(\frac{B}{r}\right),$$

then
$$A > \frac{sB}{r}, \qquad \text{[Prop. 7.}$$

$$\therefore rA > sB.$$

If
$$A = s\left(\frac{B}{r}\right),$$

then
$$A = \frac{sB}{r},$$

$$\therefore rA = sB.$$

If
$$A < s\left(\frac{B}{r}\right),$$

then
$$A < \frac{sB}{r},$$

$$\therefore rA < sB.$$

Art. 22. AXIOM.

If A and B are two magnitudes of the same kind, it is always possible to find a multiple of either which will exceed the other.

This is usually known as the Axiom of Archimedes. But Euclid uses it in the Fifth Book, see Euc. v. 8, and it is also implied in the fourth definition of the Fifth Book.

Art. 23. PROPOSITION VIII.

If X, Y, Z be three magnitudes of the same kind and if
$$X > Y + Z,$$

to prove that an integer t exists such that
$$X > tZ > Y.$$

Let sZ be the greatest multiple of Z which does not exceed Y.

Then either   (i) $Y = sZ$

or   (ii) $sZ < Y < (s+1)Z.$

In case (i) $Y = sZ,$

$$\therefore Y < (s+1)Z,$$

but $X > Y + Z,$

$$\therefore X > (s+1)Z,$$

$$\therefore X > (s+1)Z > Y.$$

Hence $(s+1)$ is the integer required.

In case (ii)

$$Y < (s+1)Z,$$

$$X > Y + Z,$$

but

$$Y > sZ,$$

$$\therefore X > sZ + Z,$$

$$\therefore X > (s+1)Z,$$

$$\therefore X > (s+1)Z > Y.$$

Hence $(s+1)$ is the integer required.

Art. 24. EXAMPLE 8.

If X, Y, Z be three magnitudes of the same kind, and if X and Y be unequal, prove that it is always possible to find integers n and t, such that tZ lies between nX and nY.

Art. 25. An illustration of the preceding example is given in Fig. 1 in the case where X, Y, Z are segments of straight lines.

Here OA and OB are the same multiples of X and Y, such that AB is greater than Z, and OC is a multiple of Z, which is greater than OA, but less than OB.

It should be noticed that $2Z$ lies between $3X$ and $3Y$,

that $3Z$ lies between $4X$ and $4Y$,

but this is ascertained only after the figure has been drawn, whilst the fact that a multiple of Z, which in this case is $4Z$, lies between $5X$ and $5Y$ is determinable from the consideration that $5(Y-X) > Z$.

Art. 26. EXAMPLES.

9. If X, Y, Z be three magnitudes of the same kind, and if no multiple of Z can be found which is intermediate in magnitude between the same multiples of X and Y, then X and Y must be equal.

10. If $X = 4$, $Y = 5$, $Z = 6$, find from a figure the least value of n for which a single multiple of Z is intermediate in magnitude between nX and nY.

Find also the least value of n for which two multiples of Z are intermediate in magnitude between nX and nY.

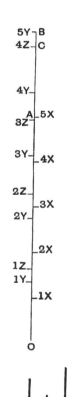

Fig. 1.

11.*   (i)   If $rA > sB,$

and $rC = sD,$

prove that integers n, t exist such that

$$nrA > tB,$$

and $$nrC < tD.$$

(ii)   If $rA = sB,$

and $rC < sD,$

prove that integers n, t exist such that

$$nrA > tB,$$

$$nrC < tD.$$

SECTION II.

Art. 27. *Def.* 2. MEASURE.

If a magnitude A contains another magnitude B an exact number of times, B is said to be a measure of A.

Art. 28. *Def.* 3. COMMON MEASURE.

If the magnitudes A and B each contain another magnitude G an exact number of times, then G is said to be a common measure of A and B.

Art. 29. *Def.* 4. COMMENSURABLE MAGNITUDES.

If two magnitudes have a common measure they are said to be commensurable.

Art. 30. ON COMMENSURABLE MAGNITUDES.

If there be two magnitudes B and C, each of which is a multiple of A, viz. :—

$$B = rA,$$
$$C = sA,$$

then the ratio of B to C is defined to be the rational fraction $\dfrac{r}{s}$.

Consequently the ratio of C to B is the rational fraction $\dfrac{s}{r}$.

Thus the value of the ratio of B to C is independent of the magnitude of their common measure A, but it does depend on the order in which the magnitudes B and C are taken.

Art. 31.   NOTATION FOR RATIO.

If two magnitudes of the same kind be called A and B, then the ratio of A to B is written $A : B$, and A is called the antecedent or first term of the ratio, whilst B is called the consequent or second term of the ratio.

If $$B = rA, \ C = sA,$$

then $$B : C = \frac{r}{s}.$$

$$\therefore \ rA : sA = \frac{r}{s}.$$

Putting A equal to unity, it follows that

$$r : s = \frac{r}{s}.$$

Consequently $$rA : sA = r : s.$$

In this book, the fact that one ratio $A : B$ is equal to another ratio $C : D$ will be expressed thus :—

$$A : B = C : D,$$

and not as it is written in most modern editions of Euclid :—

$$A : B :: C : D,$$

which is read :—

the ratio of A to B is the same as the ratio of C to D,

or more briefly, A is to B as C to D.

Art. 32.   *Def.* 5.   THE RATIO OF EQUALITY.

If in the preceding Article, both r and s be put equal to 1, then it follows that

$$A : A = 1.$$

Each of two equal magnitudes is said to have to the other the ratio of equality.

Art. 33.   *Def.* 6.   PROPORTION.

If there are four magnitudes such that the ratio of the first magnitude to the second is the same as that of the third magnitude to the fourth, then the four magnitudes are said to be proportionals, or in proportion.

If A, B, C, D are four magnitudes, such that

$$A : B = C : D,$$

then A, B, C, D are proportionals.

A and D are called the extremes of the proportion.

B and C are called the means of the proportion.

D is called the fourth proportional to A, B and C.

The antecedents A and C of the two equal ratios are said to be *corresponding**
terms of the ratios; so also are the consequents B and D.

The case in which the means of the proportion are equal to one another requires
special notice.

If $$X : Y = Y : Z,$$

then the three magnitudes X, Y, Z are said to be in proportion; Y is said to
be a mean proportional between X and Z, and Z is said to be a third proportional
to X and Y.

Art. 34.   PROPOSITION IX.

ENUNCIATION.   *Two parallelograms, situated between the same parallels, have
commensurable bases, to prove that the ratio of the area of the first parallelogram
to the area of the second parallelogram is equal to the ratio of the base of the first
parallelogram to the base of the second parallelogram.*

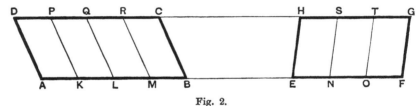

Fig. 2.

Let the parallelograms $ABCD, EFGH$ have their bases AB, EF commensurable.

Let AK be a common measure of AB, EF.

Suppose that $$AB = r (AK),$$
and that $$EF = s (AK).$$

Let AB, EF be divided as in the figure into parts each equal to AK, and
through the points of division let straight lines be drawn parallel to the sides
AD, CB of the parallelogram $ABCD$; and to the sides EH, FG of the parallelogram
$EFGH$, so that each parallelogram is divided up into equal parallelograms.

Then since the bases of all these parallelograms are equal, and they are
situated between the same parallels, they are equal in area.

Since AB contains r lengths each equal to AK, therefore the parallelogram
$ABCD$ contains r parallelograms each equal to $AKPD$,

$$\therefore \ ABCD = r (AKPD).$$

* Euclid uses the term 'homologous.'

Also $$EF = s\,(EN) = s\,(AK).$$
Thus EF contains s lengths each equal to AK, therefore the parallelogram $EFGH$ contains s parallelograms each equal to $AKPD$,
$$\therefore\ EFGH = s\,(AKPD).$$
Since $$AB = r\,(AK),$$
$$EF = s\,(AK),$$
$$\therefore\ AB : EF = \frac{r}{s}.$$
Since $$ABCD = r\,(AKPD),$$
and $$EFGH = s\,(AKPD),$$
$$\therefore\ ABCD : EFGH = \frac{r}{s}.$$
$$\therefore\ ABCD : EFGH = AB : EF.$$

In the same way it can be shown that

If two triangles have the same altitude, and have commensurable bases, the ratio of the area of the first triangle to the area of the second triangle is equal to the ratio of the base of the first triangle to the base of the second triangle.

Art. 35. A particular example of this proposition is the following. If a side of a square be divided into ten equal parts, and perpendiculars be drawn to the side through the points of division, the square will be divided into ten equal rectangles; and the area of each rectangle will be one-tenth of the area of the square.

If the side of the square be divided into a hundred equal parts, and perpendiculars be drawn to the side through the points of division, the square will be divided into a hundred equal rectangles, and the area of each rectangle will be one-hundredth of the area of the square; and so on.

Art. 36. The preceding proposition is sufficient to render it possible to calculate approximately the area of any rectilineal figure.

Take the rectilineal figure $ABCDE$. (Fig. 3.)

Join BD.

Draw CF parallel to BD to meet AB produced at F.

Then $\triangle BDF = \triangle BDC$, since they are on the same base BD and between the same parallels BD, FC.

Add to each the figure $ABDE$.

$$\therefore\ ABDE + \triangle BDF = ABDE + \triangle BDC.$$
$$\therefore\ AFDE = ABCDE.$$

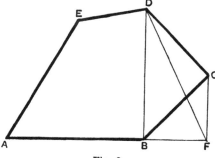

Fig. 3.

Now join *FE*. (Fig. 4.)

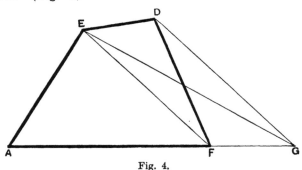

Fig. 4.

Draw *DG* parallel to *EF* to meet *AF* produced at *G*.

Then △*FED* = △*FEG*, since they are on the same base *FE* and between the same parallels *FE* and *DG*.

Add to each the △*AFE*.

$$\therefore\ \triangle AFE + \triangle FED = \triangle AFE + \triangle FEG.$$
$$\therefore\ AFDE = \triangle AEG.$$

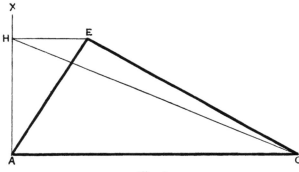

Fig. 5.

Through *A* (Fig. 5), draw a perpendicular *AX* to *AG*, and through *E* draw *EH* parallel to *AG* to meet *AX* at *H*.

Join *GH*.

Then △*AEG* = △*AHG*, for they are on the same base *AG* and between the same parallels.

Hence
$$ABCDE = AFDE$$
$$= \triangle AEG$$
$$= \triangle AHG.$$

Hence a right-angled triangle AHG has been constructed having the same area as the given rectilineal figure $ABCDE$.

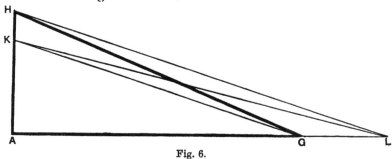

Fig. 6.

Now let AK (Fig. 6) be taken along AH equal to the unit of length, say one inch.

Join KG.

Draw HL parallel to KG to meet AG produced in L.

Join KL.

Then $\triangle KHG = \triangle KGL$, since they are on the same base KG and between the same parallels KG, HL.

Add to each $\triangle AKG$.

$$\therefore\ \triangle AKG + \triangle KHG = \triangle AKG + \triangle KGL.$$
$$\therefore\ \triangle AHG = \triangle AKL.$$
$$\therefore\ \triangle AKL = ABCDE.$$

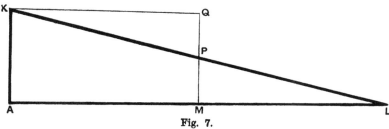

Fig. 7.

Now bisect KL at M. (Fig. 7.)

Through M draw a perpendicular to AL, to meet KL at P, and produce it to Q, until $PQ = MP$.

Now since M is the mid-point of AL, and MP is parallel to AK, therefore P is the mid-point of KL, and MP is half of AK.

Then $MQ = 2MP = AK.$

Thus MQ is equal and parallel to AK.

$$\therefore\ AMQK \text{ is a parallelogram,}$$

and since $K\hat{A}M$ is a right angle,

$$\therefore AMQK \text{ is a rectangle.}$$

Also
$$MP = PQ,$$
$$PL = PK,$$
$$M\hat{P}L = Q\hat{P}K,$$
$$\therefore \text{ the triangles } MPL, QPK \text{ are congruent,}$$
$$\therefore \triangle MPL = \triangle QPK.$$

Add to each $AMPK$,
$$\therefore AMPK + \triangle MPL = AMPK + \triangle QPK,$$
$$\therefore \triangle ALK = AMQK.$$

Hence a rectangle $AMQK$ has been constructed, whose area is equal to that of $ABCDE$, and which has one side AK equal to the unit of length.

If now there be measured off consecutive units of length along AM as long as this is possible, and then tenths of units as long as this is possible, and then hundredths of units as long as this is possible, and so on, and if through the points of division parallels be drawn to AK, then it follows from Art. 35 that $AMQK$ contains as many units and fractions of units of area as AM contains units and fractions of units of length.

Art. 37.   LEMMA.

If two intersecting straight lines OX, OY be cut by four parallel straight lines AE, BF, CG, DH; and if $AB = CD$, then must $EF = GH$.

Draw EJ parallel to OX to meet BF at J, and draw GK parallel to OX to meet DH at K.

Since $AEJB$ is a parallelogram,
$$\therefore EJ = AB.$$

Since $CGKD$ is a parallelogram,
$$\therefore GK = CD,$$
but
$$AB = CD,$$
$$\therefore EJ = GK.$$

Now consider the triangles EJF, GKH.

In these triangles

$EJ = GK$.

$E\hat{F}J = G\hat{H}K, \quad \because BF \text{ is parallel to } DH.$

$F\hat{E}J = H\hat{G}K, \quad \because EJ \text{ is parallel to } GK.$

Hence the triangles are congruent.
$$\therefore EF = GH.$$

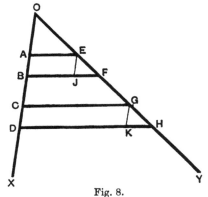

Fig. 8.

Art. 38. PROPOSITION X. (Euc. VI. 9.)

ENUNCIATION. *To divide a finite segment of a straight line into any number of equal parts.*

It is required to divide the segment OA into r equal parts.

Through O draw any straight line OX.

On it set off any length OB, and then measure off consecutive lengths each equal to OB, until a point G is reached such that $OG = r\,(OB)$.

Join AG, and through the points of division of OG draw parallels to AG.

These parallels will divide OA into r equal parts by the lemma of Art. 37.

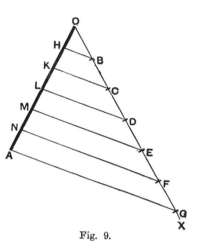

Fig. 9.

Art. 39. *Def.* 7. CORRESPONDING POINTS AND SEGMENTS ON TWO STRAIGHT LINES.

When two straight lines are cut by a single system of parallel straight lines, it is convenient to call the two points, in which one of the parallel straight lines cuts the two straight lines, *corresponding* **points; and to call the segments of the two straight lines between any pair of the parallel straight lines** *corresponding* **segments.**

Note. If the two straight lines intersect, the point of intersection on one straight line will correspond to itself on the other straight line.

Art. 40. PROPOSITION XI.

ENUNCIATION. *If two straight lines be cut by any number of parallel straight lines, to prove that the ratio of any two commensurable segments of one line is equal to the ratio of the corresponding segments of the other line.*

Let OX, OY be the two straight lines cut by the parallels AE, BF, CG, DH, and suppose that the segments AB, CD have a common measure AK.

Let
$$AB = r\,(AK),$$
$$CD = s\,(AK).$$

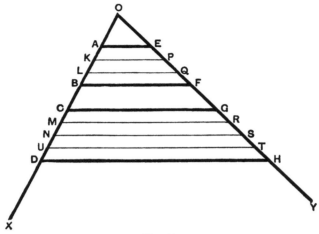

Fig. 10.

Then AB may be divided into r equal parts AK, KL, LB; and CD may be divided into s equal parts CM, MN, NU, UD.

Through the points of division K, L, M, N, U draw parallels to AE to cut OY at P, Q, R, S, T respectively.

Then it follows from Art. 37 that

$$EP = PQ = QF = GR = RS = ST = TH,$$

and since AB is divided into r pieces, each equal to AK, therefore EF is divided into r pieces each equal to EP. This will be stated shortly thus* :—

Since
$$AB = r\,(AK),$$
$$\therefore \ EF = r\,(EP),$$

and since
$$CD = s\,(CM) = s\,(AK),$$
$$\therefore \ GH = s\,(GR) = s\,(EP).$$
$$\therefore \ AB : CD = r\,(AK) : s\,(AK)$$
$$= \frac{r}{s},$$
$$EF : GH = r\,(EP) : s\,(EP)$$
$$= \frac{r}{s},$$
$$\therefore \ AB : CD = EF : GH.$$

* Similar abbreviations in the argument are used below in this and some subsequent propositions.

Art. 41. PROPOSITION XII.

ENUNCIATION. *In the same circle or in equal circles the ratio of two commensurable angles at the centre is equal to the ratio of the arcs on which they stand.*

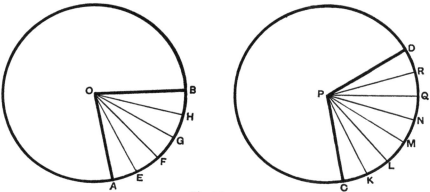

Fig. 11.

Let AOB, CPD be angles at the centre of two equal circles having the angle AOE as a common measure.

Let $A\hat{O}B = r(A\hat{O}E).$

Let $C\hat{P}D = s(A\hat{O}E).$

Then the angle AOB is divisible into the r angles $A\hat{O}E$, $E\hat{O}F$, $F\hat{O}G$, $G\hat{O}H$, $H\hat{O}B$ each equal to $A\hat{O}E$; and the angle $C\hat{P}D$ is divisible into the s angles $C\hat{P}K$, $K\hat{P}L$, $L\hat{P}M$, $M\hat{P}N$, $N\hat{P}Q$, $Q\hat{P}R$, $R\hat{P}D$ each equal to $A\hat{O}E$.

Now in equal circles, equal angles at the centre stand on equal arcs.

∴ the arcs EF, FG, GH, HB are each equal to the arc AE; and since

$$A\hat{O}B = r(A\hat{O}E),$$

∴ arc $AB = r$ (arc AE).

Similarly ∵ $C\hat{P}D = s(C\hat{P}K) = s(A\hat{O}E),$

∴ arc $CD = s$ (arc CK) $= s$ (arc AE).

Now $A\hat{O}B : C\hat{P}D = r(A\hat{O}E) : s(A\hat{O}E)$

$$= \frac{r}{s},$$

arc $AB :$ arc $CD = r$ (arc AE) $: s$ (arc AE)

$$= \frac{r}{s},$$

∴ $A\hat{O}B : C\hat{P}D =$ arc $AB :$ arc CD.

SECTION III.

Art. 42. Let there be two magnitudes of the same kind, A and B.

Suppose that A is an exact multiple of G, say aG; and that B is also an exact multiple of G, say bG.

Then the ratio of A to B has been defined to be the rational fraction $\dfrac{a}{b}$.

Take now another multiple of G, say cG, and let $C = cG$.

The ratio of C to B is $\dfrac{c}{b}$.

Now if
$$C > A,$$
$$cG > aG,$$
$$\therefore\ c > a,$$
$$\therefore\ \frac{c}{b} > \frac{a}{b},$$
$$\therefore\ C:B > A:B.$$

Hence if $C > A$, then $C:B > A:B$.

Next if
$$C = A,$$
$$cG = aG,$$
$$\therefore\ c = a,$$
$$\therefore\ \frac{c}{b} = \frac{a}{b},$$
$$\therefore\ C:B = A:B.$$

$\therefore$ if $C = A$, then $C:B = A:B.$

Next if
$$C < A,$$
$$cG < aG,$$
$$c < a,$$
$$\frac{c}{b} < \frac{a}{b},$$
$$\therefore \ C : B < A : B.$$

Hence if $C < A$, then $C : B < A : B$.

There are therefore the three propositions

    (1) If $C > A$, then $C : B > A : B$.

    (2) If $C = A$, then $C : B = A : B$.

    (3) If $C < A$, then $C : B < A : B$.

The meaning of these is easily grasped if they are written out with fewer symbols.

Thus the second says that equal magnitudes have the same ratio to a third magnitude.

The first says that if C be greater than A, then C has a greater ratio to B than A has.

The third is not essentially distinct from the first.

The converse propositions to the above will next be proved.   These are

    (4) If $C : B > A : B$, then $C > A$.

    (5) If $C : B = A : B$, then $C = A$.

    (6) If $C : B < A : B$, then $C < A$.

  Take (4).

Suppose that $C : B > A : B$,

then one of the following alternatives must hold,

$$C > A, \ \text{ or } \ C = A, \ \text{ or } \ C < A.$$

Now if $C = A$, then by (2) $C : B = A : B$ which is contrary to the hypothesis.

And if $C < A$, then by (3) $C : B < A : B$ which is contrary to the hypothesis.

Hence C is not equal to A, nor less than A, and therefore C is greater than A.

Propositions (5) and (6) depend on (1), (2), (3) in the same way.

Consequently (4), (5) and (6) are logical deductions from (1), (2) and (3).

Art. 43. The proofs of (1), (2), (3) of the preceding article depend on the fact that A, B, C are integral multiples of the same magnitude G.

It will be necessary however in what follows to deal with the ratios of magnitudes which have no common measure.

Now the definition given for the ratio of magnitudes having a common measure is not applicable to magnitudes which have no common measure.

Two alternatives therefore present themselves.

Either two magnitudes, which have no common measure, cannot be said to have a ratio;

or the definition of ratio must be extended so as to apply to the case of two magnitudes which have no common measure.

The latter alternative will be selected.

In the first place it is clear that the ratio of magnitudes having no common measure is not expressible as a rational fraction.

Before it can be explained what is meant by the ratio of two magnitudes which have no common measure, it is necessary to extend the idea of number, by defining the irrational number. It will then appear that the ratio of two magnitudes which have no common measure is an irrational number. This subject is treated more at length in the Appendix, but here it will be enough to say that the irrational number is a magnitude *of the same kind* (in the technical sense in which these words are used in Art. 21) as the rational fraction. Hence it is supposed to be possible to determine whether any irrational number is less than or greater than any given rational number, whatever that given rational number may be. Whenever this is possible the irrational number is considered to be known.

In order to construct a theory of the ratios of magnitudes which have no common measure, it will be assumed that the propositions

$$\text{if } C > A, \text{ then } C:B > A:B;$$
$$\text{if } C = A, \text{ then } C:B = A:B;$$
$$\text{and if } C < A, \text{ then } C:B < A:B$$

hold good whether A, B, C have a common measure or not.

From these as explained in Art. 42, it follows

$$\text{that if } C:B > A:B, \text{ then } C > A;$$
$$\text{if } C:B = A:B, \text{ then } C = A;$$
$$\text{and if } C:B < A:B, \text{ then } C < A.$$

From the above propositions the following will be deduced.

Art. 44. PROPOSITION XIII.

To prove that

$$(1) \quad \text{If } A : B > \frac{n}{r}, \text{ then } rA > nB.$$

$$(2) \quad \text{If } A : B = \frac{n}{r}, \text{ then } rA = nB.$$

$$(3) \quad \text{If } A : B < \frac{n}{r}, \text{ then } rA < nB.$$

And conversely, $$(4) \quad \text{If } rA > nB, \text{ then } A : B > \frac{n}{r}.$$

$$(5) \quad \text{If } rA = nB, \text{ then } A : B = \frac{n}{r}.$$

$$(6) \quad \text{If } rA < nB, \text{ then } A : B < \frac{n}{r}.$$

(These propositions are very important and will be used repeatedly in what follows.)

To prove (1).   It is assumed* that a magnitude Q exists such that $B = rQ$.

Further by definition $\qquad nQ : rQ = \dfrac{n}{r}.$

Now, by hypothesis, $\qquad\qquad A : B > \dfrac{n}{r},$

$$\therefore A : rQ > nQ : rQ,$$
$$\therefore A > nQ, \qquad\qquad\qquad\qquad \text{[Art. 43.}$$
$$\therefore rA > rnQ,$$
$$\therefore rA > n\,(rQ),$$
$$\therefore rA > nB.$$

To prove (2).   Here, by hypothesis,

$$A : B = \frac{n}{r},$$
$$\therefore A : B = nQ : rQ.$$

But $\qquad\qquad\qquad\qquad B = rQ,$
$$\therefore A : rQ = nQ : rQ,$$
$$\therefore A = nQ, \qquad\qquad\qquad\qquad \text{[Art. 43.}$$
$$\therefore rA = r\,(nQ) = n\,(rQ) = nB.$$

* It is not necessary to be able to construct Q. All that is assumed is that Q exists.

To prove (3). Here, by hypothesis,

$$A : B < \frac{n}{r},$$

$$\therefore A : B < nQ : rQ,$$

$$\therefore A : rQ < nQ : rQ,$$

$$\therefore A < nQ,$$ [Art. 43.

$$\therefore rA < r(nQ),$$

$$\therefore rA < n(rQ),$$

$$\therefore rA < nB.$$

To prove (4). Here, by hypothesis,

$$rA > nB.$$

Take

$$B = rQ,$$

$$\therefore rA > n(rQ),$$

$$\therefore rA > r(nQ),$$

$$\therefore A > nQ;$$

$$\therefore A : rQ > nQ : rQ,$$ [Art. 43.

$$\therefore A : B > \frac{n}{r}.$$

To prove (5). Here, by hypothesis,

$$rA = nB,$$

$$B = rQ,$$

$$rA = n(rQ) = r(nQ),$$

$$A = nQ;$$

$$\therefore A : B = nQ : rQ = \frac{n}{r}.$$ [Art. 43.

To prove (6). Here, by hypothesis,

$$rA < nB.$$

$$\therefore rA < n(rQ),$$

$$\therefore rA < r(nQ),$$

$$\therefore A < nQ,$$

$$\therefore A : rQ < nQ : rQ,$$ [Art. 43.

$$\therefore A : B < nQ : rQ;$$

$$\therefore A : B < \frac{n}{r}.$$

Art. 45. It is now possible to find approximate values for the ratios of quantities which have no common measure.

Let A and B have no common measure.

Assume that a quantity Q exists such that $B = rQ$.

Now A is not a multiple of Q, for if it were A and B would have a common measure, Q.

Consequently some integer s exists such that sQ is less than A, but $(s+1)Q$ is greater than A.

Since

$$A > sQ,$$
$$\therefore A : B > sQ : B, \qquad \text{[Art. 43.}$$
$$\therefore A : B > sQ : rQ,$$
$$\therefore A : B > \frac{s}{r}.$$

Since

$$A < (s+1)Q,$$
$$\therefore A : B < (s+1)Q : B, \qquad \text{[Art. 43.}$$
$$\therefore A : B < (s+1)Q : rQ;$$
$$\therefore A : B < \frac{s+1}{r}.$$

Hence the ratio of A to B lies between

$$\frac{s}{r} \quad \text{and} \quad \frac{s+1}{r}.$$

The difference of these two fractions is $\frac{1}{r}$, which can be made as small as we please, by sufficiently increasing r. This is possible, on the hypothesis made that, B being given, and any integer whatever r taken, a quantity Q exists such that

$$B = rQ.$$

In this way an approximate measure of the ratio of any two magnitudes of the same kind can be obtained.

But it is not enough to decide the important question whether two given ratios are or are not equal.

If each can only be measured approximately, it still remains possible for their difference to be less than the degree of accuracy of measurement.

Art. 46. ON EQUAL RATIOS.

Two ratios are equal if no rational fraction lies between them.

Now if no rational fraction lies between $A : B$ and $C : D$, then if any rational fraction whatever $\frac{s}{r}$ be selected, and it be found that $A : B$ is greater than $\frac{s}{r}$, then $C : D$ must also be greater than $\frac{s}{r}$; if however $A : B$ is equal to $\frac{s}{r}$, then

$C : D$ must also be equal to $\frac{s}{r}$; but if $A : B$ is less than $\frac{s}{r}$, then $C : D$ must also be less than $\frac{s}{r}$.

These conditions must be satisfied for every value of the integers r, s.

The conditions, written more shortly are

$$\text{If } A : B > \frac{s}{r}, \text{ then must } C : D > \frac{s}{r};$$

$$\text{If } A : B = \frac{s}{r}, \text{ then must } C : D = \frac{s}{r};$$

$$\text{If } A : B < \frac{s}{r}, \text{ then must } C : D < \frac{s}{r},$$

whatever values the integers r, s may have.

By Prop. 13 these conditions are equivalent to the following.

If r, s be any integers whatever, and

  if all values of r, s which make $rA > sB$, also make $rC > sD$......(1);

  if all values of r, s which make $rA = sB$, also make $rC = sD$......(2);

  if all values of r, s which make $rA < sB$, also make $rC < sD$......(3),

then $A : B = C : D.$

These are the conditions given by Euclid in the Fifth Definition of the Fifth Book for the equality of the ratios $A : B$ and $C : D$.

The three sets of conditions given above may be called collectively the Test for the Equality of two Ratios*.

Art. 47.   They may be replaced by equivalent conditions in various ways†.

One of these is as follows:—

If r, s be any integers whatever, and

  if $rC > sD$, then must $rA > sB$; ....(4)

  if $rC = sD$, then must $rA = sB$; ....(5)

  if $rC < sD$, then must $rA < sB$. ....(6)

To show that this is so, let it be supposed that (1), (2) and (3) hold.

If possible let some values of r, s exist, such that

$$rC > sD, \text{ but } rA \ngtr sB.$$

Then either $rA = sB$, or $rA < sB$.

---

* See Note 3.   † See Prop. 14 and Examples 12 and 13 in Art. 50.

If $rA = sB$, then by (2) $rC = sD$,

and if $rA < sB$, then by (3) $rC < sD$,

both of which are contrary to the hypothesis that $rC > sD$.

Hence $rA > sB$, and $\therefore$ (4) holds.

In like manner (5) and (6) can be proved.

The most important result in regard to the conditions (1), (2) and (3) is this, that (2) is included in (1) and (3)*. This is proved in Proposition 14.

Art. 48. PROPOSITION XIV.

To prove that if all values of r, s which make

$$rA > sB, \text{ also make } rC > sD \quad \dots\dots\dots\dots\dots\dots(1),$$

and if all values of r, s which make

$$rA < sB, \text{ also make } rC < sD \quad \dots\dots\dots\dots\dots\dots(3),$$

then if any values of r, s exist which make $rA = sB$, they also make $rC = sD$.

Suppose that when $r = r_1$, $s = s_1$,

$$rA = sB,$$

but

$$rC \neq sD,$$

i.e.

$$r_1 A = s_1 B,$$

but either

$$r_1 C > s_1 D$$

or

$$r_1 C < s_1 D.$$

Suppose first

$$r_1 C > s_1 D.$$

Then $r_1 C - s_1 D$ is a magnitude of the same kind C or D.

Hence by Archimedes' Axiom an integer n exists, such that

$$n(r_1 C - s_1 D) > D\dagger,$$

$$\therefore nr_1 C > (ns_1 + 1)D,$$

but

$$r_1 A = s_1 B,$$

$$\therefore nr_1 A = ns_1 B,$$

$$\therefore nr_1 A < (ns_1 + 1)B.$$

Now putting $r = nr_1$, $s = ns_1 + 1$ in (3) it follows that as

$$nr_1 A < (ns_1 + 1)B$$

---

* The first explicit mention of this result known to the author is in Stolz's *Vorlesungen über Allgemeine Arithmetik*, Part I. p. 87, published in 1885.

† The proof may be completed by taking $n(r_1 C - s_1 D) > C$.

it is necessary to have
$$nr_1C < (ns_1 + 1)\,D,$$
which is contrary to what has been proved above that
$$nr_1C > (ns_1 + 1)\,D.$$

Hence r_1C is not greater than s_1D.

Take next the case
$$r_1C < s_1D.$$

Then $s_1D - r_1C$ is a magnitude of the same kind as C or D.

Hence by Archimedes' Axiom an integer n exists such that
$$n\,(s_1D - r_1C) > C^*,$$
$$\therefore\ ns_1D > (nr_1 + 1)\,C,$$
i.e. $$(nr_1 + 1)\,C < ns_1D.$$

But $$r_1A = s_1B,$$
$$\therefore\ nr_1A = ns_1B,$$
$$\therefore\ (nr_1 + 1)\,A > ns_1B.$$

Now putting $r = nr_1 + 1$, $s = ns_1$ in (1), it follows that as
$$(nr_1 + 1)\,A > ns_1B,$$
then must $$(nr_1 + 1)\,C > ns_1D,$$
which is contrary to what has been shown above that
$$(nr_1 + 1)\,C < ns_1D.$$

Hence r_1C is not less than s_1D.

It was proved before that
$$r_1C \text{ is not greater than } s_1D.$$

Consequently $$r_1C = s_1D.$$

It follows therefore that there is no need to consider the set of conditions (2). In fact this set of conditions is never satisfied unless the magnitudes concerned are commensurable.

For if $rA = sB$, and if a magnitude Q be taken such that $B = rQ$, then
$$rA = s\,(rQ) = r\,(sQ),$$
$$\therefore\ A = sQ.$$

Thus A and B have a common measure Q.

Although it is not necessary to consider the set of conditions (2), this will nevertheless be done in many of the proofs which follow, because in the comparison

* The proof may be completed by taking $n\,(s_1D - r_1C) > D$.

of any ratio with any rational fraction there are always three alternatives to be considered, and the consideration of the alternative corresponding to the condition (2) is sometimes instructive, and does not involve any additional difficulty.

It follows therefore *that in order to prove that* $A : B = C : D$, *it is sufficient and necessary to show that*

if $$A : B > \frac{s}{r}, \text{ then } C : D > \frac{s}{r},$$

and if $$A : B < \frac{s}{r}, \text{ then } C : D < \frac{s}{r},$$

whatever integers r, s *may be.*

Art. 49. UNEQUAL RATIOS.

In connection with Euclid's Test for Equal Ratios, it is interesting to consider his test for distinguishing the greater of two unequal ratios from the smaller.

It is as follows:—

If $\qquad\qquad$ rA be greater than sB,

but $\qquad\qquad$ rC be not greater than sD,

then $\qquad\qquad$ $A : B > C : D.$

$\quad$ Now if $\qquad\qquad$ $rA > sB$,

then $\qquad\qquad$ $A : B > \dfrac{s}{r}$;

and if $\qquad\qquad$ $rC \not> sD$,

then $\qquad\qquad$ $C : D \not> \dfrac{s}{r}.$

Hence $\qquad\qquad$ $A : B$ is greater than $\dfrac{s}{r}$,

but $\qquad\qquad$ $C : D$ is not greater than $\dfrac{s}{r}.$

Consequently $\qquad\qquad$ $A : B$ is greater than $C : D.$

Notice that the conditions are equivalent to either

$$rA > sB, \qquad rC = sD,$$

or $\qquad$ $$rA > sB, \qquad rC < sD,$$

each of which is inconsistent with the conditions laid down in the Test for Equal Ratios.

Art. 50.   EXAMPLES.

12.* If all values of r, s which make $rA > sB$, also make $rC > sD$, and if all values of r, s which make $rC > sD$, also make $rA > sB$, prove that $A : B = C : D$.

13.* If all values of r, s which make $rA < sB$, also make $rC < sD$, and if all values of r, s which make $rC < sD$, also make $rA < sB$, prove that $A : B = C : D$.

14. If for a *single* value of the integer r, say r_1, and a *single* value of the integer s, say s_1, it is true that

$$r_1 A = s_1 B$$

and $$r_1 C = s_1 D,$$

then prove that *any* values of the integers r, s which make

(1) $rA > sB$, also make $rC > sD$,

(2) $rA = sB$, also make $rC = sD$,

(3) $rA < sB$, also make $rC < sD$.

15.   If $rA < sB,$

if $rC > sE,$

if $tA > uB,$

if $tC < uF;$

and if further $A : B = C : D,$

prove that $E < D < F.$

SECTION IV.

PROPOSITIONS 15—26.

THE SIMPLER PROPOSITIONS IN THE THEORY OF RATIOS WITH GEOMETRICAL APPLICATIONS.

Art. 51. **PROPOSITION XV.** (Euc. V. 15.)

To prove that $\qquad A : B = nA : nB.$

Take any rational fraction $\dfrac{s}{r}$.

If $\qquad\qquad\qquad\qquad A : B > \dfrac{s}{r},$

then $\qquad\qquad\qquad\qquad rA > sB,$ $\qquad\qquad$ [Prop. 13.

$$\therefore\ n(rA) > n(sB);$$

$$\text{i.e. } r(nA) > s(nB);$$

$$\therefore\ nA : nB > \dfrac{s}{r}.$$ $\qquad\qquad$ [Prop. 13.

But if $\qquad\qquad\qquad\qquad A : B < \dfrac{s}{r},$

then $\qquad\qquad\qquad\qquad rA < sB,$ $\qquad\qquad$ [Prop. 13.

$$\therefore\ n(rA) < n(sB),$$

$$\text{i.e. } r(nA) < s(nB),$$

$$\therefore\ nA : nB < \dfrac{s}{r}.$$ $\qquad\qquad$ [Prop. 13.

Hence it has been shown

$$\text{if } A : B > \dfrac{s}{r}, \text{ then } nA : nB > \dfrac{s}{r},$$

but $\qquad\quad \text{if } A : B < \dfrac{s}{r}, \text{ then } nA : nB < \dfrac{s}{r}.$

Hence by Art. 48

$$A : B = nA : nB*.$$

The case of the above Proposition in which $n = 2$ will often be required,

i.e. $A : B = 2A : 2B.$

Since n represents any whole number whatever, it may have an infinite number of values.

Hence nA and nB represent an infinite number of pairs of magnitudes, e.g. $2A$ and $2B$, $3A$ and $3B$, ... such that the ratio of any pair is the same as that of A, B.

Hence there are an infinite number of pairs of magnitudes which have the same ratio.

Hence if a ratio be given, the magnitudes of which it is the ratio are not given.

Thus two magnitudes of the same kind determine a definite ratio; but if a ratio only be given, the magnitudes of which it is the ratio are not determined.

Art. 52. PROPOSITION XVI. (Euc. VI. 1.)

ENUNCIATION. *The ratio of the areas of two parallelograms (or triangles) which have the same altitude is equal to the ratio of the lengths of their bases.*

Any two parallelograms which have the same altitude may be placed so as to lie between the same parallels.

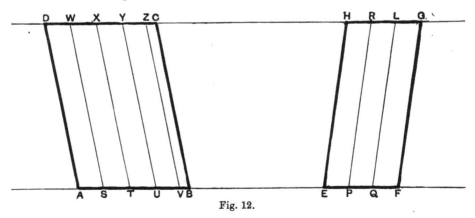

Fig. 12.

Let $ABCD$, $EFGH$ be two parallelograms lying between the same parallels.

---

* If A and B are numbers, then denoting numbers by small letters it follows that

$$a : b = na : nb.$$

It is required to prove that

$$AB : EF = ABCD : EFGH.$$

Take any rational fraction $\frac{s}{r}$.

The ratio $AB : EF$ will be compared with this fraction.

Cut EF into r equal parts EP, PQ, QF.

Set off s consecutive lengths AS, ST, TU, UV each equal to EP along AB.

Then $AV = s (EP).$

Then three alternatives are possible:

$$(i) \quad AB > AV;$$
$$(ii) \quad AB = AV;$$
$$(iii) \quad AB < AV.$$

Through P, Q draw parallels to EH, FG; and through S, T, U, V draw parallels to AD.

Then the parallelograms $EPRH$, $PQLR$, $QFGL$ are equal, and the parallelogram $EFGH$ is equal to r times the parallelogram $EPRH$.

In like manner,

$$AVZD = s (ASWD) = s (EPRH).$$

Now take case (i), (Fig. 12), $AB > AV$.

$$\therefore \ AB : EF > AV : EF \qquad\qquad\qquad \text{[Art. 43.}$$
$$> s (EP) : r (EP)$$
$$> \frac{s}{r};$$

but since $AB > AV,$

$$\therefore \ ABCD > AVZD;$$
$$\therefore \ ABCD : EFGH > AVZD : EFGH \qquad\qquad \text{[Art. 43.}$$
$$> s (EPRH) : r (EPRH)$$
$$> \frac{s}{r}.$$

It has therefore been shown that,

if $AB : EF > \dfrac{s}{r},$

then $ABCD : EFGH > \dfrac{s}{r}.$

Next take case (ii), $\qquad AB = AV.$

In this case V falls on B,

and the parallelograms $AVZD$, $ABCD$ are the same,

$$\because \; AB = AV,$$

$$\therefore \; AB : EF = AV : EF \qquad\qquad \text{[Art. 43.}$$

$$= s\,(EP) : r\,(EP)$$

$$= \frac{s}{r}.$$

Also $\qquad\qquad\qquad ABCD = AVZD;$

$$\therefore \; ABCD : EFGH = AVZD : EFGH \qquad\qquad \text{[Art. 43.}$$

$$= s\,(EPRH) : r\,(EPRH)$$

$$= \frac{s}{r}.$$

It has therefore been shown that,

if $\qquad\qquad\qquad AB : EF = \dfrac{s}{r},$

then $\qquad\qquad ABCD : EFGH = \dfrac{s}{r}.$

Lastly take the case (iii), (Fig. 13), $AB < AV.$

In this case the figure has the following form.

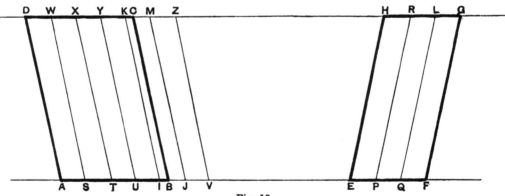

Fig. 13.

Here $\qquad\qquad\qquad AB < AV,$

$$AB : EF < AV : EF \qquad\qquad \text{[Art. 43.}$$

$$< s\,(EP) : r\,(EP)$$

$$< \frac{s}{r}.$$

But since $$AB < AV,$$

$$\therefore \ ABCD < AVZD;$$

$$\therefore \ ABCD : EFGH < AVZD : EFGH \qquad \text{[Art. 43.}$$

$$< s(EPRH) : r(EPRH)$$

$$< \frac{s}{r}.$$

It has therefore been shown that

$$\text{if } AB : EF < \frac{s}{r}, \text{ then } ABCD : EFGH < \frac{s}{r};$$

and it was previously shown that

$$\text{if } AB : EF = \frac{s}{r}, \text{ then } ABCD : EFGH = \frac{s}{r},$$

but $$\text{if } AB : EF > \frac{s}{r}, \text{ then } ABCD : EFGH > \frac{s}{r}.$$

Putting these results together it follows by Art. 46 that

$$AB : EF = ABCD : EFGH.$$

Art. 53.   EXAMPLES.

16.   Given two rectilineal areas, and a straight line, find another straight line such that the ratio of the areas is the same as that of the lines.

17.   Given two straight lines, and a rectilineal area, find another rectilineal area such that the ratio of the lines is the same as that of the areas.

18.   Given three rectilineal areas, find a fourth such that the ratio of the first to the second area is the same as that of the third to the fourth.

19.   Prove that the ratio of the areas of two triangles on equal bases is the same as the ratio of their altitudes.

20.   If ABC be a triangle, and O any point in its plane, and if AO cut BC at D, prove that

$$BD : DC = \triangle AOB : \triangle AOC.$$

Art. 54.   PROPOSITION XVII.   (Containing the first part of Euc. VI. 2.)

ENUNCIATION.   *If two straight lines be cut by any number of parallel straight lines, to prove that the ratio of any two segments of one line is equal to that of the corresponding segments of the other line.*

Let the intersecting lines OX, OY be cut by the parallel straight lines AB, CD, EF, GH.

Then the segment AC corresponds to the segment BD,

and   the segment EG corresponds to the segment FH.

It is required to prove that $AC : EG = BD : FH$.

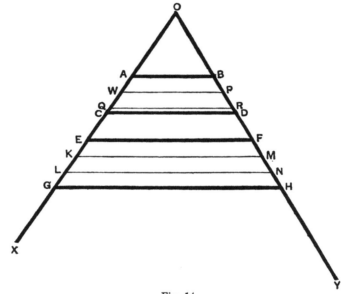

Fig. 14.

Take any rational fraction $\dfrac{s}{r}$.

Divide EG into r equal parts, EK, KL, LG.

From A set off s consecutive lengths, each equal to EK, along AC.

Let $AQ = s\,(EK)$.

Three cases are possible :

(i) $AQ < AC$,

(ii) $AQ = AC$,

(iii) $AQ > AC$.

(i)   Through the points of division K, L, W, Q draw parallels to AB.

Then by Art. 37 $FM = MN = NH = BP = PR$,

$$\therefore FH = r\,(FM) = r\,(BP),$$

$$BR = s\,(BP).$$

In figure 14 $AC > AQ$,

$$\therefore AC : EG > AQ : EG \qquad\qquad\qquad \text{[Art. 43.}$$

$$> s\,(EK) : r\,(EK)$$

$$> \frac{s}{r}.$$

Again from the figure,

since $AC > AQ$,

and AB, QR, CD are parallel,

$$\therefore BD > BR,$$

$$\therefore BD : FH > BR : FH \qquad\qquad\qquad \text{[Art. 43.}$$

$$> s\,(BP) : r\,(BP)$$

$$> \frac{s}{r}.$$

It is therefore proved that

if $AC : EG > \dfrac{s}{r}$,

then $BD : FH > \dfrac{s}{r}$.

(ii)   In this case Q falls on C,

and therefore R falls on D,

$$AC = s\,(EK), \qquad EG = r\,(EK),$$

$$BD = s\,(BP), \qquad FH = r\,(BP);$$

$$\therefore AC : EG = \frac{s}{r}$$

and $BD : FH = \dfrac{s}{r}$.

It is therefore proved that if $AC : EG = \dfrac{s}{r}$, then $BD : FH = \dfrac{s}{r}$.

(iii)   In this case (Fig. 15) $AC < AQ$,

$$\therefore AC : EG < AQ : EG \qquad \text{[Art. 43.}$$

$$< s\,(EK) : r\,(EK)$$

$$< \frac{s}{r}.$$

In this case $AC < AQ$,

and AB, QR, CD are parallel,

$$\therefore BD < BR,$$

$$\therefore BD : FH < BR : FH \qquad \text{[Art. 43.}$$

$$< s\,(BP) : r\,(BP)$$

$$< \frac{s}{r}.$$

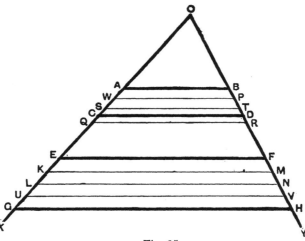

Fig. 15.

It is therefore proved that if $AC : EG < \dfrac{s}{r}$,

then $BD : FH < \dfrac{s}{r}$.

Putting the three cases together, it follows by Art. 46 that

$$AC : EG = BD : FH.$$

Art. 55.   COROLLARY.

As a particular case of the preceding, it follows that *if ABC be a triangle, and if the sides AB, AC be cut by any straight line parallel to BC, then the sides AB, AC are divided proportionally.*

Let *DE*, parallel to *BC*, cut *AB* at *D* and *AC* at *E*.
There are three varieties of figure.

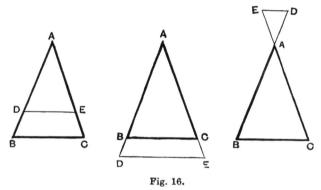

Fig. 16.

The point	*A*	corresponds to the point			*A*
,, ,,	*B*	,,	,,	,,	*C*
,, ,,	*D*	,,	,,	,,	*E*
The segment	*AB*	,,	,,	segment	*AC*
,, ,,	*AD*	,,	,,	,,	*AE*
,, ,,	*BD*	,,	,,	,,	*CE.*

From the above, by means of Proposition 17, the following results may be deduced, the first being the one most frequently required.

$$AD : DB = AE : EC.$$
$$DB : AD = EC : AE.$$
$$AB : AD = AC : AE.$$
$$AD : AB = AE : AC.$$
$$AB : BD = AC : CE.$$
$$BD : AB = CE : AC.$$

These six results are not independent.

Any one of them being given, the rest follow as consequences by means of the properties of ratio as will be seen hereafter.

Art. 56. PROPOSITION XVIII. (Euc. VI. 12.)

ENUNCIATION. *To find a fourth proportional to three given straight lines**.
Let *AB*, *CD*, *EF* be three straight lines.

* My attention was called to the construction here given by the late Mr Budden.

It is required to find a straight line OL, such that $AB : CD = EF : OL$.

Then OL is called the fourth proportional to AB, CD, EF.

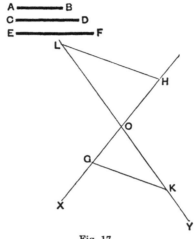

Fig. 17.

Let OX, OY be two straight lines intersecting at O; measure off on OX in opposite directions $OG = AB$, $OH = CD$.

On OY measure off $OK = EF$.

Join GK, and draw HL parallel to GK, meeting OY at L.

Then the intersecting lines OX, OY are cut by the parallels GK, HL.

The points G, O, H correspond to K, O, L respectively.

The segments GO, OH correspond to KO, OL respectively.

$$\therefore\ GO : OH = KO : OL, \qquad\qquad \text{[Prop. 17.}$$
$$\therefore\ AB : CD = EF : OL.$$

Art. 57.   EXAMPLE 21.

Given three straight lines AB, CD, EF, it is required to construct another straight line P such that

$$P : AB = CD : EF,$$
or
$$AB : P = CD : EF,$$
or
$$AB : CD = P : EF.$$

Art. 58.   DEFINITION 8.

If in the figure of proposition 18

$$CD = EF,$$

then OL is such that
$$AB : CD = CD : OL,$$
and OL is called the third proportional to AB and CD.

Art. 59. EXAMPLE 22.

In the triangle ABC, a straight line DE is drawn parallel to BC cutting AB at D and AC at E. DF is drawn parallel to BE, cutting AC at F.

Prove that AF is a third proportional to AC and AE.

Art. 60. *Def.* 9. SIMILARLY DIVIDED STRAIGHT LINES.

Two straight lines are said to be similarly divided, when the ratio of any two parts of one straight line is the same as that of the two corresponding parts of the other straight line.

Art. 61. PROPOSITION XIX. (Euc. VI. 10.)

ENUNCIATION. *To divide a straight line similarly to a given divided straight line.*

It is required to divide the given straight line AB similarly to the way in which the line CF is divided at D and E.

Through A draw any straight line AX (not in the same straight line as AB), and on it measure off $AG = CD$, $GH = DE$, $HK = EF$.

Join BK, and draw GL, HM parallel to BK cutting AB in L, M respectively.

Then since GL, HM, BK are parallel lines, the segments AG, AL correspond; so do GH, LM; and HK, MB.

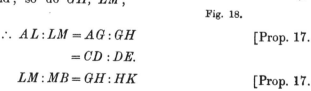

Fig. 18.

$$\therefore AL : LM = AG : GH$$

[Prop. 17.

$$= CD : DE.$$

Also
$$LM : MB = GH : HK$$

[Prop. 17.

$$= DE : EF,$$

and so on.

Hence AB is divided similarly to CF.

Art. 62. PROPOSITION XX. (Euc. VI. 33.)

ENUNCIATION. *In the same circle or in equal circles*

(i)   *angles at the centre are proportional to the arcs on which they stand.*

(ii) *angles at the circumference are proportional to the arcs on which they stand.*

(iii) *angles at the centre are proportional to the sectors bounded by the sides of the angles and the arcs on which they stand.*

If the angles are in the same circle, the figure may be drawn twice over, so that it is sufficient to consider the case where there are two equal circles.

(i) Let A, B, Figs. 19—24, be the centres of two equal circles.

Let CAD, EBF be two angles at the centres standing on the arcs CD, EF.

It is required to prove that

$$C\hat{A}D : E\hat{B}F = \text{arc } CD : \text{arc } EF.$$

Let the fraction $\dfrac{s}{r}$ be compared with the ratio

$$C\hat{A}D : E\hat{B}F.$$

There are three alternatives:

$$(1)\quad C\hat{A}D : E\hat{B}F > \frac{s}{r};$$

$$(2)\quad C\hat{A}D : E\hat{B}F = \frac{s}{r};$$

$$(3)\quad C\hat{A}D : E\hat{B}F < \frac{s}{r}.$$

Make $C\hat{A}G$ equal to $r(C\hat{A}D)$, then since equal angles at the centre of a circle stand on equal arcs it follows that

$$\text{the arc } CG = r(\text{arc } CD).$$

Make next $E\hat{B}H$ equal to $s(E\hat{B}F)$, then

$$\text{the arc } EH = s\,(\text{arc } EF).$$

In case (i), see Figs. 19 and 20.

$$\because \ C\hat{A}D : E\hat{B}F > \frac{s}{r},$$

$$r\,(C\hat{A}D) > s\,(E\hat{B}F); \qquad\qquad \text{[Prop. 13.}$$

$$\therefore\; C\hat{A}G > E\hat{B}H\,;$$

$$\therefore\;\text{arc } CG > \text{arc } EH^*\,;$$

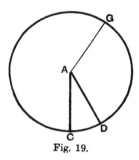

Fig. 19.

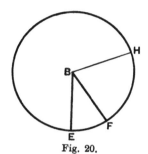

Fig. 20.

$$\therefore\; r\,(\text{arc } CD) > s\,(\text{arc } EF)\,;$$

$$\therefore\;\text{arc } CD : \text{arc } EF > \frac{s}{r}\,. \qquad\qquad\text{[Prop. 13.}$$

In case (ii), see Figs. 21 and 22.

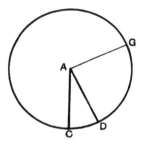

Fig. 21.

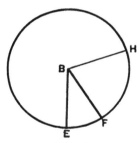

Fig. 22.

$$C\hat{A}D : E\hat{B}F = \frac{s}{r}\,;$$

$$\therefore\; r\,(C\hat{A}D) = s\,(E\hat{B}F)\,; \qquad\qquad\text{[Prop. 13.}$$

$$\therefore\; C\hat{A}G = E\hat{B}H\,;$$

$$\therefore\;\text{arc } CG = \text{arc } EH\,;$$

$$\therefore\; r\,(\text{arc } CD) = s\,(\text{arc } EF)\,;$$

$$\therefore\;\text{arc } CD : \text{arc } EF = \frac{s}{r}\,. \qquad\qquad\text{[Prop. 13.}$$

* This follows immediately from the proposition that in equal circles equal angles at the centres stand on equal arcs.

In case (iii), see Figs. 23 and 24.

$$C\hat{A}D : E\hat{B}F < \frac{s}{r}\,;$$

$$\therefore\ r(C\hat{A}D) < s(E\hat{B}F)\,;$$ [Prop. 13.

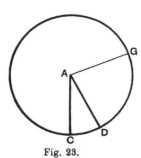

Fig. 23.   Fig. 24.

$$\therefore\ C\hat{A}G < E\hat{B}H\,;$$

$$\therefore\ \text{arc } CG < \text{arc } EH*\,;$$

$$\therefore\ r(\text{arc } CD) < s(\text{arc } EF)\,;$$

$$\therefore\ \text{arc } CD : \text{arc } EF < \frac{s}{r}\,.$$ [Prop. 13.

Hence   if $C\hat{A}D : E\hat{B}F > \dfrac{s}{r}\,,$

then arc CD : arc $EF > \dfrac{s}{r}\,;$

if $C\hat{A}D : E\hat{B}F = \dfrac{s}{r}\,,$

then arc CD : arc $EF = \dfrac{s}{r}\,;$

and if $C\hat{A}D : E\hat{B}F < \dfrac{s}{r}\,,$

then arc CD : arc $EF < \dfrac{s}{r}\,.$

$$\therefore\ C\hat{A}D : E\hat{B}F = \text{arc } CD : \text{arc } EF.$$ [Art. 46.

* This follows immediately from the proposition that in equal circles equal angles at the centres stand on equal arcs.

(ii)   An angle at the centre of a circle is double the angle at the circumference standing on the same arc.

Hence the ratio of two angles at the centre of the same or of equal circles is the same as that of the angles at the circumference on the same arcs.   [Art. 51.

Hence, by case (i), the ratio of two angles at the circumference of the same or of equal circles is the same as that of the arcs on which they stand.

(iii)   The proof of this is derivable from that of (i) by replacing therein each arc by the corresponding sector.

Art. 63.   *Def.* 10.   RECIPROCAL RATIOS.

The ratios $A : B$ and $B : A$ are called reciprocal ratios.

Art. 64.   EXAMPLE 23.

If two reciprocal ratios are equal, prove that each of them is a ratio of equality.

Art. 65.   PROPOSITION XXI.   (Corollary to Euc. V. 4.)*

ENUNCIATION.   *If two ratios are equal their reciprocal ratios are equal,* i.e. *if* $A : B = C : D,$

to prove that $B : A = D : C.$

Compare the ratio $B : A$ with the rational number $\dfrac{s}{r}$.

By Art. 48 it is necessary to consider only the alternatives

$$\text{(1)}\quad B : A > \frac{s}{r},$$

$$\text{(2)}\quad B : A < \frac{s}{r}.$$

In case (1) $B : A > \dfrac{s}{r}$;

$$\therefore\ rB > sA\ ;\qquad\qquad\text{[Prop. 13.}$$
$$\therefore\ sA < rB\ ;$$

$$\therefore\ A : B < \frac{r}{s}\ ;\qquad\qquad\text{[Prop. 13.}$$

but $A : B = C : D$;

$$\therefore\ C : D < \frac{r}{s}\ ;$$

$$\therefore\ sC < rD\ ;\qquad\qquad\text{[Prop. 13.}$$

* Simson numbers this proposition Euc. V. B.

$$\therefore\ rD > sC\ ;$$

$$\therefore\ D : C > \frac{s}{r}\ .$$ [Prop. 13.

In case (2) $$B : A < \frac{s}{r}\ ;$$

$$\therefore\ rB < sA\ ;$$ [Prop. 13.

$$\therefore\ sA > rB\ ;$$

$$\therefore\ A : B > \frac{r}{s}\ ;$$ [Prop. 13.

but $$A : B = C : D\ ;$$

$$\therefore\ C : D > \frac{r}{s}\ ;$$

$$\therefore\ sC > rD\ ;$$ [Prop. 13.

$$\therefore\ rD < sC\ ;$$

$$\therefore\ D : C < \frac{s}{r}\ .$$ [Prop. 13.

Hence if $B : A > \frac{s}{r}$, then $D : C > \frac{s}{r}$;

but if $B : A < \frac{s}{r}$, then $D : C < \frac{s}{r}$.

$$\therefore\ B : A = D : C.$$ [Art. 48.

Art. 66. PROPOSITION XXII. (Euc. V. 7, 2nd Part.)

ENUNCIATION. *If A, B, C be three magnitudes of the same kind, and if A be equal to B, then*

$$C : A = C : B.$$

If A be equal to B, then by Art. 43

$$A : C = B : C\ ;$$

$$\therefore\ C : A = C : B.$$ [Prop. 21.

Art. 67. PROPOSITION XXIII. (Euc. V. 9, 2nd Part.)

ENUNCIATION. *If A, B, C be three magnitudes of the same kind, and if*

$$C : A = C : B,$$

then $$A = B.$$

Now if $$C : A = C : B,$$

then $$A : C = B : C\ ;$$ [Prop. 21.

$$\therefore\ A = B.$$ [Art. 43.

Art. 68.   EXAMPLE 24.

(i)   If $rA : B = sA : C$, prove that $sB = rC$.

(ii) If $A : rC = B : sC$, prove that $sA = rB$.

Art. 69.   PROPOSITION XXIV.   (Euc. V. 16.)*

ENUNCIATION.   *If A, B, C, D be four magnitudes of the same kind, and if $A : B = C : D$, to prove that $A : C = B : D$.*

Compare the ratio $A : C$ with any rational fraction $\dfrac{s}{r}$.

By Art. 48 it is necessary to consider only the two alternatives

$$(1)\quad A : C > \frac{s}{r},$$

$$(2)\quad A : C < \frac{s}{r}.$$

In case (1), $A : C > \dfrac{s}{r}$,

$$rA > sC.\qquad\qquad\qquad\text{[Prop. 13.}$$

Hence $rA - sC$ is a magnitude of the same kind as A, B, C, D.

Comparing it with B†, then by Archimedes' Axiom (Art. 22) an integer n exists such that

$$n(rA - sC) > B,$$
$$\therefore\ nrA - nsC > B,$$
$$\therefore\ nrA > nsC + B.$$

Hence a multiple of B, say tB, exists such that

$$nrA > tB > nsC.\qquad\qquad\text{[Prop. 8.}$$
$$\because\ nrA > tB,$$
$$\therefore\ A : B > \frac{t}{nr},\qquad\qquad\text{[Prop. 13.}$$

but $A : B = C : D$,

$$\therefore\ C : D > \frac{t}{nr},$$
$$\therefore\ nrC > tD\qquad\text{(I)},\qquad\qquad\text{[Prop. 13.}$$

* See Note 6.   † The reader should complete the proof by taking D instead of B.

but
$$tB > nsC \qquad \text{(II)},$$

$$\therefore\ snrC > stD \quad \text{from (I)},$$

and
$$rtB > rnsC \ \text{from (II)},$$

$$\therefore\ rtB > stD,$$

$$\therefore\ rB > sD^*,$$

$$\therefore\ B:D > \frac{s}{r}. \qquad\qquad \text{[Prop. 13.}$$

In case (2),
$$A:C < \frac{s}{r},$$

$$rA < sC. \qquad\qquad \text{[Prop. 13.}$$

Hence $sC - rA$ is a magnitude of the same kind as A, B, C, D.

Comparing it with $B\dagger$, then by Archimedes' Axiom an integer n exists such that

$$n(sC - rA) > B,$$

$$\therefore\ nsC > nrA + B.$$

Hence (by Prop. 8) a multiple of B, say tB, exists such that

$$nsC > tB > nrA.$$

$$\because\ nrA < tB,$$

$$\therefore\ A:B < \frac{t}{nr}, \qquad\qquad \text{[Prop. 13.}$$

but
$$A:B = C:D,$$

$$\therefore\ C:D < \frac{t}{nr},$$

$$\therefore\ nrC < tD \qquad \text{(III)}, \qquad\qquad \text{[Prop. 13.}$$

but
$$nsC > tB \qquad \text{(IV)},$$

$$\therefore\ snrC < stD \quad \text{from (III)},$$

$$rnsC > rtB \ \text{from (IV)},$$

$$\therefore\ rtB < stD,$$

$$\therefore\ rB < sD,$$

$$\therefore\ B:D < \frac{s}{r}. \qquad\qquad \text{[Prop. 13.}$$

---

* This result is an algebraic consequence of the inequalities (I and II). It is obtained by transforming them so that the multiple of C (which is the magnitude appearing in both) becomes the same in each.

† The reader should complete the proof by taking D instead of B.

Hence it has been proved that

if
$$A : C > \frac{s}{r}, \text{ then } B : D > \frac{s}{r};$$

and if
$$A : C < \frac{s}{r}, \text{ then } B : D < \frac{s}{r}.$$

$$\therefore A : C = B : D.$$ [Art. 48.

Art. 70. COROLLARY. (Euc. V. 14.)

If A, B, C, D are all magnitudes of the same kind, and if
$$A : B = C : D,$$
then $A \gtreqless C$, according as $B \gtreqless D$, and conversely.

Since $A : B = C : D$, and the magnitudes are all of the same kind,

$$\therefore A : C = B : D.$$ [Prop. 24.

Compare now the ratio $B : D$ with the rational fraction $\frac{1}{1}$.

If
$$B : D > \frac{1}{1},$$

then
$$B > D.$$ [Prop. 13.

Since
$$B : D = A : C,$$

$$\therefore A : C > \frac{1}{1},$$

$$\therefore A > C.$$ [Prop. 13.

The other cases may be proved in the same way.

Art. 71. EXAMPLES.

25. If
$$A : B = C : D,$$
if
$$E : C = F : A,$$
if
$$E : D = F : G,$$
and if the magnitudes A, B, C, D, E, F, G are all of the same kind, prove that $B = G$.

[The proposition is also true if A, B, F, G are of the same kind, and if C, D, E are of the same kind, as may be proved by using Prop. 37 below.]

26. If A, B, C, D are four points on a straight line such that B divides AC internally in the same ratio as D divides it externally; prove that C divides BD internally in the same ratio as A divides it externally.

Art. 72. *Def.* 11. HARMONIC POINTS.

Four points A, B, C, D **on a straight line are said to be four harmonic points if** B **and** D **divide** AC **in the same ratio, one internally and the other externally.**

Then A and C are called conjugate points; as are also B and D.

Art. 73. **PROPOSITION XXV.** (Euc. VI. 2, 2nd Part.)

ENUNCIATION. *If two sides of a triangle are divided proportionally so that the segments terminating at the vertex common to the two sides correspond to each other, then the straight line joining the points of division is parallel to the other side.*

Let the points D and E divide the sides AB, AC of the triangle ABC, so that

$$AD : DB = AE : EC,$$

then will DE be parallel to BC.

If DE be not parallel to BC, draw BF parallel to DE cutting AC at F.

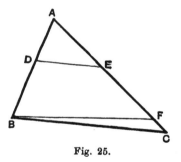

Fig. 25.

$$AD : DB = AE : EF, \qquad \text{[Prop. 17.}$$
$$\therefore \; AE : EC = AE : EF,$$
$$\therefore \; EC = EF, \qquad\qquad \text{[Art. 43.}$$

which is impossible.

Hence DE is parallel to BC.

Art. 74. EXAMPLE 27.

If $ABCD$ be a plane quadrilateral, and if E, F, G, H be points on AB, BC, CD, DA respectively such that

$$AE : AB = CF : CB = CG : CD = AH : AD,$$

prove that $EFGH$ is a parallelogram.

Art. 75. PROPOSITION XXVI.*

ENUNCIATION. (1) *A given segment of a straight line can be divided internally into segments having the ratio of one given line to another in one way only.*

(2) *A given segment of a straight line can be divided externally into segments having the ratio of one given line to any other not equal to it in one way only.*

(1) Let AB be the straight line to be divided internally at some point C, so that

$$AC : CB = K : L,$$

where K, L are two given segments of straight lines.

Through A, one of the extremities of AB, draw any straight line AX, and measure off AD equal to K, and DE equal to L in the *same* direction as AD.

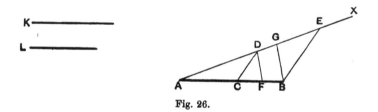

Fig. 26.

Join BE, and through D draw DC parallel to EB, cutting AB at C. Then C will divide AB, so that $AC : CB = K : L$.

Since AB, AX are cut by the parallel lines CD, BE; the segments AC, CB correspond respectively to AD, DE.

$$\therefore\ AC : CB = AD : DE \qquad\qquad \text{[Prop. 17.}$$
$$= K : L.$$

Hence C is one point which satisfies the required condition.

If possible let F be some other point which also satisfies the required condition.

Join FD, and draw BG parallel to FD cutting AE at G.

* See Note 7.

Then the segments AF, FB correspond to AD, DG respectively.

$$\therefore\ AF : FB = AD : DG,\qquad\qquad\text{[Prop. 17.}$$

but by hypothesis $\qquad\qquad AF : FB = K : L.$

$$\therefore\ AD : DG = K : L$$

$$= AD : DE.$$

$$\therefore\ DG = DE,\qquad\qquad\text{[Art. 43.}$$

which is impossible.

Hence C is the only point which satisfies the required condition.

It is important to notice that if $K < L$, then $AC < CB$, and C is nearer to A than to B.

If $K = L$, then $AC = CB$, and C is the middle point of AB.

If $K > L$, then $AC > CB$, and C is further from A than from B.

These three cases correspond to different figures in the second part of the proposition.

(2) In this case the figures differ from that of the first case in having the length DE (equal to L) measured in the *opposite* direction to AD; and that is the only difference in the *constructions* for the cases $K < L$, $K > L$.

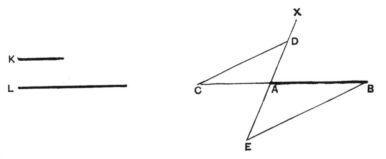

Fig. 27.

If $K < L$, then E must fall on DA produced through A as in Fig. 27, and C is nearer to A than to B.

If $K > L$, then E must fall between D and A, as in Fig. 28, and C is further from A than from B.

The *proofs* for the cases $K < L$ and $K > L$ are the same as in Case (1). They need not therefore be repeated.

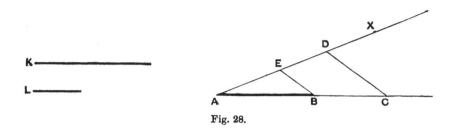

Fig. 28.

Art. 76. NOTE ON CASE (2) OF THE PRECEDING ARTICLE.

If $K = L$, E coincides with A.

Hence BE coincides with BA.

Hence the parallel through D to BE is parallel to BA, as in Fig. 29.

Hence in this case from Euclid's point of view the construction fails, and there is no point corresponding to C.   See Note 7.

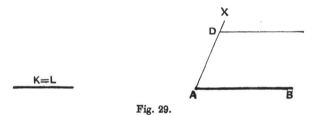

Fig. 29.

SECTION V.

PROPOSITIONS 27—34.

SIMILAR FIGURES.

Art. 77. *Def.* 12.

Similar rectilineal figures are those which satisfy the following two sets of conditions.

(1) The angles of one of the figures taken in order must be respectively equal to the angles of the other figure taken in order.

(2) Those sides in the two figures which join the vertices of equal angles being defined as corresponding sides, the ratio of any pair of corresponding sides must be equal to the ratio of every other pair of corresponding sides.

Let $A_1B_1C_1D_1E_1$, $A_2B_2C_2D_2E_2$ be two similar figures, then the two sets of conditions are as follows :—

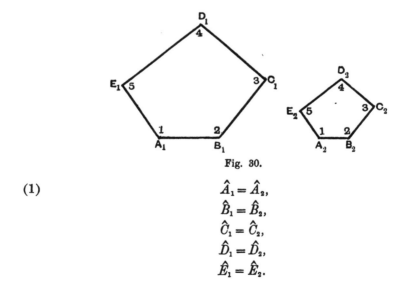

Fig. 30.

(1)
$$\hat{A}_1 = \hat{A}_2,$$
$$\hat{B}_1 = \hat{B}_2,$$
$$\hat{C}_1 = \hat{C}_2,$$
$$\hat{D}_1 = \hat{D}_2,$$
$$\hat{E}_1 = \hat{E}_2.$$

(As there is in this figure only one angle at each vertex it is sufficient to indicate each angle by the letter standing at its vertex.)

It is often convenient to indicate the equality of two angles in two similar rectilineal figures by marking the equal angles with the same number, e.g. in the above figures the equal angles at A_1, A_2 are both marked 1.

(2)   Since $\hat{A}_1 = \hat{A}_2,$

and $\hat{B}_1 = \hat{B}_2,$

∴ the side A_1B_1 corresponds to the side A_2B_2.

In like manner B_1C_1 corresponds to B_2C_2, and so on.

$$\therefore \; A_1B_1 : A_2B_2 = B_1C_1 : B_2C_2 = C_1D_1 : C_2D_2 = D_1E_1 : D_2E_2 = E_1A_1 : E_2A_2.$$

Art. 78. *Def.* 13.

The ratio of a side of the first figure to the corresponding side of the second figure is called the ratio of similitude of the first figure to the second.

Art. 79. Note. It is obvious that two congruent figures are similar to one another. For such figures the ratio of similitude is the ratio of equality.

Art. 80. Similar figures are said to be *similarly described* on two straight lines, when these two straight lines are corresponding sides of the figures, e.g. :—

The figures $A_1B_1C_1D_1E_1$, $A_2B_2C_2D_2E_2$ are similarly described on A_1B_1, A_2B_2 ; or on B_1C_1, B_2C_2 ; and so on.

(In general language two similar figures are similarly described on two straight lines to which they have the same relation.)

Art. 81.   EXAMPLE 28.

If B be the middle point of AC, and BX, CY be drawn perpendicular to AC, and if A be joined to any point P on BX, and if on AP on the side remote from B a triangle APQ be described similar to ABP so that the sides AP, PQ of APQ may correspond to the sides AB, BP of ABP, prove that Q is equidistant from A and from the straight line CY.

Art. 82. PROPOSITION XXVII. (Euc. VI. 21.)

ENUNCIATION. *Rectilineal figures which are similar to the same rectilineal figure are similar to one another.*

Let the figure $ABCD$ be similar to $A_1B_1C_1D_1$, and also to $A_2B_2C_2D_2$, it is required to prove that $A_1B_1C_1D_1$ and $A_2B_2C_2D_2$ are similar to each other.

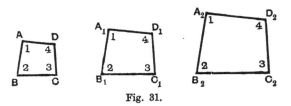

Fig. 31.

Since $ABCD$ is similar to $A_1B_1C_1D_1$

$$\therefore \ \hat{A} = \hat{A}_1, \ \hat{B} = \hat{B}_1, \ \hat{C} = \hat{C}_1, \ \hat{D} = \hat{D}_1 \ \dots\dots\dots\dots\dots(1)$$

$$AB : A_1B_1 = BC : B_1C_1 = CD : C_1D_1 = DA : D_1A_1 \ \dots\dots\dots\dots(2).$$

Since $ABCD$ is similar to $A_2B_2C_2D_2$

$$\therefore \ \hat{A} = \hat{A}_2, \ \hat{B} = \hat{B}_2, \ \hat{C} = \hat{C}_2, \ \hat{D} = \hat{D}_2 \ \dots\dots\dots\dots\dots(3)$$

$$AB : A_2B_2 = BC : B_2C_2 = CD : C_2D_2 = DA : D_2A_2 \ \dots\dots\dots\dots(4).$$

From (1) and (3) it follows that

$$\hat{A}_1 = \hat{A}_2, \ \hat{B}_1 = \hat{B}_2, \ \hat{C}_1 = \hat{C}_2, \ \hat{D}_1 = \hat{D}_2 \ \dots\dots\dots\dots\dots(5).$$

From (2) $\qquad\qquad AB : A_1B_1 = BC : B_1C_1,$

$$\therefore \ AB : BC = A_1B_1 : B_1C_1. \qquad\qquad \text{[Prop. 24.}$$

Similarly from (4) $\qquad\quad AB : BC = A_2B_2 : B_2C_2$

$$\therefore \ A_1B_1 : B_1C_1 = A_2B_2 : B_2C_2$$

$$\therefore \ A_1B_1 : A_2B_2 = B_1C_1 : B_2C_2. \qquad\qquad \text{[Prop. 24.}$$

In like manner it can be shown that

$$B_1C_1 : B_2C_2 = C_1D_1 : C_2D_2 = D_1A_1 : D_2A_2.$$

$$\therefore \ A_1B_1 : A_2B_2 = B_1C_1 : B_2C_2 = C_1D_1 : C_2D_2 = D_1A_1 : D_2A_2 \ \dots\dots\dots(6).$$

Now (5) and (6) are the two sets of conditions which must be satisfied in order that $A_1B_1C_1D_1$ and $A_2B_2C_2D_2$ may be similar (see Art. 77).

Hence $A_1B_1C_1D_1$ and $A_2B_2C_2D_2$ are similar.

Art. 83. ON SIMILAR TRIANGLES.

The different cases, in which two triangles are similar, correspond to some extent to the cases in which two triangles are congruent.

For this reason the cases in which two triangles are congruent will first be enumerated.

Art. 84. *Two triangles are congruent if*

(1) The three sides of one triangle are respectively equal to the three sides of the other triangle.

(2 *a*)* Two sides and the included angle of one triangle are respectively equal to two sides and the included angle of the other triangle.

(3 *a*)† Two angles and the adjacent side of one triangle are respectively equal to two angles and the adjacent side in the other triangle.

(3 *b*)† One side, the opposite angle, and one other angle of one triangle are respectively equal to one side, the opposite angle, and one other angle in the other triangle.

Besides the above cases there should be noted the following, in which three elements (sides or angles) of one triangle are respectively equal to the three corresponding elements of the other triangle, viz. those in which

(2 *b*)* One angle, the opposite side, and one other side of one triangle are respectively equal to one angle, the opposite side and one other side of the other triangle.

In this case the angles opposite the other pair of equal sides are either equal or supplementary, and in the former alternative the triangles are congruent.

(This case is usually known as the Ambiguous Case.)

(4) Three angles of one triangle are respectively equal to three angles of the other triangle.

This last case is only mentioned in order to complete all the possible cases in which three elements of one triangle are respectively equal to the three corresponding elements of another triangle. In it the triangles are not generally congruent, but are always similar (see Prop. 28).

Art. 85. To case (1) above corresponds the proposition that if the sides of one triangle taken in order are proportional to the sides of another triangle taken in order, then the triangles are similar.

---

* The numbers attached to the cases (2 *a*) and (2 *b*) both contain the same number 2 because in each there are two sides and one angle given equal.

† The numbers attached to the cases (3 *a*) and (3 *b*) both contain the same number 3 because in each there are two angles and one side given equal.

To case (2 *a*) corresponds the proposition that if two sides of a triangle are proportional to two sides of another triangle, and the included angles are equal, then the triangles are similar.

To case (2 *b*) corresponds the proposition that if two triangles have one angle of the one equal to one angle of the other, and the sides about one other angle proportional in such a manner that the sides opposite the equal angles correspond, then the triangles have their remaining angles either equal or supplementary, and in the former case the triangles are similar.

To cases (3 *a*), (3 *b*) and (4), in all of which the three angles of the one triangle are respectively equal to the three angles of the other triangle, corresponds the *single* proposition that if the angles of one triangle are respectively equal to the angles of another triangle, then the triangles are similar.

Hence there are four cases of similar triangles to be dealt with.

It should be noticed that the first and last amount to the proposition that, *in the case of triangles*, if either of the two sets of conditions for the similarity of rectilineal figures be satisfied, then the other set must also be satisfied.

So that the two sets of conditions for the similarity of rectilineal figures are not independent when the rectilineal figures are triangles.

Art. 86. In dealing with similar triangles the reader will find it useful to draw the similar triangles separately if they happen to overlap, and to mark equal angles with the same numbers, as in the figure.

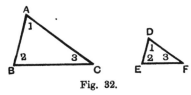

Fig. 32.

Then those sides which join the equal angles have the same numbers at their extremities, and it is therefore at once evident that they are corresponding sides.

If in the triangles *ABC*, *DEF*, $\hat{A} = \hat{D}$, $\hat{B} = \hat{E}$, and $\hat{C} = \hat{F}$, let *A* and *D* be marked 1, let *B* and *E* be marked 2, and let *C* and *F* be marked 3.

Write down all the possible pairs of the numbers 1, 2, 3, viz. :—23, 31, 12.

Now 2 and 3 are at the extremities of *BC* in one triangle, and at the extremities of *EF* in the other.

Hence *BC*, *EF* are corresponding sides.

In like manner the positions of the numbers 3 and 1 indicate that *CA*, *FD* are corresponding sides, and the positions of the numbers 1 and 2 indicate that *AB* and *DE* are corresponding sides.

$$\therefore BC : EF = CA : FD = AB : DE.$$

Art. 87.   PROPOSITION XXVIII.   (Euc. VI. 4.)

ENUNCIATION.   *If the three angles of one triangle are respectively equal to the three angles of another triangle, then the triangles are similar.*

Those sides correspond which join the vertices of equal angles.

In the triangles ABC, DEF, let

$$\hat{A} = \hat{D},$$

$$\hat{B} = \hat{E},$$

$$\hat{C} = \hat{F}.$$

To prove that the triangles are similar*.

From A on AB measure off a length AG equal to DE, and then draw GH parallel to BC cutting AC at H.

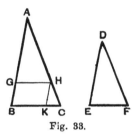

Fig. 33.

It will first be shown that the triangles AGH, DEF are congruent.

Since GH is parallel to BC,

$$A\hat{G}H = A\hat{B}C = D\hat{E}F.$$

Also $$G\hat{A}H = B\hat{A}C = E\hat{D}F,$$

and $$AG = DE.$$

Hence the triangles AGH, DEF are congruent.

$$\therefore AH = DF,$$

$$GH = EF.$$

Since GH is parallel to BC,

$$\therefore BA : GA = CA : HA.$$ [Prop. 17.

$$\therefore BA : DE = CA : DF.$$

†Now draw HK parallel to AB.

Then $$CA : HA = CB : KB.$$ [Prop. 17.

---

* Observe that if the triangles are similar, the vertex A of the triangle ABC corresponds to the vertex D of the triangle DEF;
  and the side AB of the triangle ABC corresponds to the side DE of the triangle DEF.

† It has now been shown that the sides which meet at A are proportional to the corresponding sides which meet at D.

Consequently a similar proof will show that the sides which meet at B are proportional to the corresponding sides which meet at E.

$$\therefore BA : ED = BC : EF.$$

$$\therefore AB : DE = BC : EF = CA : FD.$$

Now $BGHK$ is a parallelogram,

$$\therefore BK = GH = EF$$

and
$$HA = DF.$$

$$\therefore CA : DF = CB : EF.$$

Hence
$$BA : DE = CA : DF = CB : EF,$$

which, taking the letters in order, may be more conveniently written

$$AB : DE = BC : EF = CA : FD.$$

Now AB, DE join the vertices of equal angles, and are therefore corresponding sides.

In like manner BC corresponds to EF, and CA to FD.

But also
$$\hat{A} = \hat{D} \; ; \; \hat{B} = \hat{E} \; ; \; \hat{C} = \hat{F}.$$

Hence the two sets of conditions for the similarity of the triangles ABC, DEF are satisfied.

Hence the triangles are similar.

It should be noticed that corresponding sides of the triangles are opposite to equal angles; e.g. AB corresponds to DE, and they are opposite to the equal angles $\hat{C}$ and $\hat{F}$ respectively.

Art. 88.   COROLLARY TO PROP. 28.

If a triangle be cut by a straight line parallel to one of the sides, the triangular portion cut off is similar to the whole triangle.

For with the figure of Prop. 28, GH may be regarded as any straight line parallel to BC, the triangles AGH, ABC are equiangular, and therefore similar by Prop. 28.

Art. 89.   EXAMPLES.

29. Show how to draw a straight line across two of the sides of a triangle, but not parallel to the third side, which will cut off a triangle similar to the original triangle.

When will it be impossible to do this?

30. If ABC be a triangle inscribed in a circle, and CD a diameter of the circle, and AE a perpendicular from A on the side BC, show that the triangles AEB, ACD are similar.

Art. 90.   PROPOSITION XXIX.*   (Euc. VI. 5.)

ENUNCIATION. *If the sides taken in order of one triangle are proportional to the sides taken in order of another triangle, prove that the triangles are similar, and that those angles are equal which are opposite to corresponding sides.*

In the triangles ABC, DEF let it be given that

$$AB : DE = BC : EF = CA : FD, \qquad\qquad\text{(I)}$$

to prove that the triangles ABC, DEF are similar.

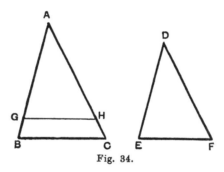

Fig. 34.

From A the vertex of the triangle ABC which corresponds to D, measure off on AB, the side corresponding to DE, a length AG equal to DE.

Draw GH parallel to BC, cutting AC at H.

It will first be shown that the triangles AGH and DEF are congruent.

The triangles AGH and ABC have the angles of the one respectively equal to the angles of the other.

Therefore by Prop. 28 they are similar.

$$\therefore\ AB : AG = BC : GH = CA : HA. \qquad\qquad\text{(II)}$$

Now $\qquad\qquad\qquad DE = AG,$

$$\therefore\ AB : DE = AB : AG. \qquad\qquad\text{[Prop. 22.}$$

Hence each of the three ratios marked (I) is equal to each of the three ratios marked (II).

$$\therefore\ BC : EF = BC : GH,$$

$$\therefore\ EF = GH. \qquad\qquad\text{[Prop. 23.}$$

* See Note 8.

Also $CA : FD = CA : HA,$

                              $\therefore FD = HA.$ [Prop. 23.

Hence in the triangles $DEF, AGH,$

$$DE = AG,$$

$$EF = GH,$$

$$FD = HA;$$

$\therefore$ they are congruent.

$$\therefore E\hat{D}F = G\hat{A}H = B\hat{A}C,$$

$$D\hat{E}F = A\hat{G}H = A\hat{B}C,$$

$$E\hat{F}D = A\hat{H}G = B\hat{C}A.$$

Hence in the triangles ABC, DEF

$$AB : DE = BC : EF = CA : FD,$$

$$\hat{A} = \hat{D}, \quad \hat{B} = \hat{E}, \quad \hat{C} = \hat{F}.$$

Hence the triangles are similar.

The equal angles $B\hat{A}C, E\hat{D}F$ are opposite the corresponding sides $BC, EF.$

The equal angles $A\hat{B}C, D\hat{E}F$ are opposite the corresponding sides $CA, FD.$

The equal angles $B\hat{C}A, E\hat{F}D$ are opposite the corresponding sides $AB, DE.$

Art. 91. NOTE ON PROPOSITION 29.

The proviso that the sides of the triangles are proportional *when taken in order* is very important.

It is quite possible for the sides of one triangle to be proportional to the sides of another without the triangles being similar.

Suppose that in the triangles $ABC, DEF,$

$$BC : CA = EF : DE,$$

and $BC : AB = FD : DE,$

then it may be proved (see Proposition 57 below) that

$$CA : AB = FD : FE.$$

But the triangles are not similar.

In the first   proportion BC corresponds to $EF.$

In the second proportion BC corresponds to $FD.$

Hence the sides of the two triangles cannot be made to correspond.

Art. 92. PROPOSITION XXX. (Euc. VI. 6.)

ENUNCIATION. *If two sides of one triangle be proportional to two sides of another triangle, and if the included angles be equal, then the triangles are similar; and those angles are equal which are opposite to corresponding sides.*

In the triangles ABC, DEF let it be given that

$$BA : AC = ED : DF,$$

and

$$B\hat{A}C = E\hat{D}F,$$

it is required to prove that the triangles are similar; and that the angles BCA, EFD opposite the corresponding sides BA, ED are equal; and that the angles ABC, DEF opposite the corresponding sides AC, DF are equal.

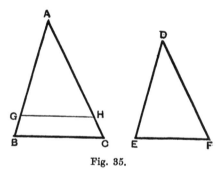

Fig. 35.

From A, the vertex of the triangle ABC which corresponds to D, measure off on AB, the side corresponding to DE, a length AG equal to DE.

Draw GH parallel to BC cutting AC at H.

It will first be proved that the triangles AGH, DEF are congruent.

Since GH is parallel to BC,

$$\therefore\ BA : GA = CA : HA, \qquad\qquad \text{[Prop. 17.}$$
$$\therefore\ BA : CA = GA : HA; \qquad\qquad \text{[Prop. 24.}$$

but it is given that $\qquad BA : CA = ED : DF$,

$$\therefore\ ED : DF = GA : HA.$$

But $\qquad\qquad ED = GA$ by construction,

$$\therefore\ DF = HA. \qquad\qquad\qquad\qquad \text{[Prop. 23.}$$

Now in the triangles DEF, AGH,

$$DE = AG,$$

$$DF = AH,$$

$$E\hat{D}F = B\hat{A}C = G\hat{A}H.$$

Hence the triangles DEF, AGH are congruent.

$$\therefore \ D\hat{E}F = A\hat{G}H = A\hat{B}C,$$

and
$$D\hat{F}E = A\hat{H}G = A\hat{C}B.$$

Hence the angles of the triangle DEF are respectively equal to the angles of the triangle ABC.

Hence by Prop. 28 the triangles DEF, ABC are similar, and those angles are equal which are opposite to corresponding sides.

Art. 93.   EXAMPLES.

31.   Two parallel straight lines are cut by any number of straight lines passing through a fixed point.

Prove that the intercepts made on the parallel lines by any two of the straight lines through the fixed point have a constant ratio.

32.   If the tangents at A and B to a circle meet at C, and if P be any point on the circle, and if PQ, PR, PS be drawn perpendicular to AC, CB, BA respectively, then prove that the triangles PAS, PBR are similar; and that the triangles PBS, PAQ are similar; and that PS is a mean proportional between PQ and PR.

33*.   If C be the centre of a circle, F any point outside it, if FA, FB be tangents to the circle at A and B respectively, if FP be any straight line through F cutting the circle at P; and if through P a straight line be drawn perpendicular to FP cutting CA at Q and CB at R; then prove that the triangles CFQ, CRF are similar; and that CF is a mean proportional between CQ and CR.

34.   Let O be the centre of a circle, and C a fixed point in its plane. Let CO cut the circle at A and B. Let P be any point on the circle, and through P let a straight line be drawn perpendicular to CP, cutting the tangents at A and B at Q and R respectively, then prove that

(1)   the triangles ACQ, BCR are similar.

(2) $AQ : AC = BC : BR$.

(3)   the angle QCR is a right angle.

Art. 94. PROPOSITION XXXI. (Euc. VI. 7.)

ENUNCIATION. *If two triangles have one angle of the one equal to one angle of the other, and the sides about one other angle in each proportional in such a manner that the sides opposite to the equal angles correspond, then the triangles have their remaining angles either equal or supplementary, and in the former case the triangles are similar.*

In the triangles ABC, DEF it is given that

$$A\hat{B}C = D\hat{E}F,$$

and

$$BA : AC = ED : DF,$$

to prove that either

(1)

$$A\hat{C}B = D\hat{F}E,$$

and the triangles ABC, DEF are similar;

or (2)

$$A\hat{C}B + D\hat{F}E = \text{two right angles*.}$$

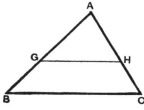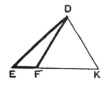

Fig. 36.

On AB, the side corresponding to DE, take a length AG equal to DE, and draw GH parallel to BC cutting AC at H.

The triangles AGH, DEF will first be compared.

Since GH is parallel to BC,

$$\therefore \ BA : GA = CA : HA, \quad\quad\quad \text{[Prop. 17.}$$
$$\therefore \ BA : CA = GA : HA. \quad\quad\quad \text{[Prop. 24.}$$

But

$$BA : CA = ED : DF,$$
$$\therefore \ ED : DF = GA : HA.$$

* Notice that the sides about the angles BAC, EDF are proportional in such a manner that the sides AC, DF opposite the equal angles ABC, DEF correspond.

Notice further that in each triangle two angles have been referred to, viz. $A\hat{B}C$, $B\hat{A}C$ in the triangle ABC and $D\hat{E}F$, $E\hat{D}F$ in the triangle DEF, and therefore the remaining angles are $A\hat{C}B$, $D\hat{F}E$.

But
$$AG = DE,$$
$$\therefore DF = HA. \qquad \text{[Prop. 23.}$$

Now in the triangles DEF, AGH,
$$DE = AG,$$
$$DF = AH,$$
$$D\hat{E}F = A\hat{B}C = A\hat{G}H,$$

where it is to be noticed that the equal angles are *opposite* to equal sides.

Now there are necessarily two alternatives,

either (1) $\qquad\qquad G\hat{A}H = E\hat{D}F,$

or (2) $\qquad\qquad G\hat{A}H$ is not equal to $E\hat{D}F.$

(1)   If $\qquad\qquad G\hat{A}H = E\hat{D}F,$

then $\qquad\qquad B\hat{A}C = E\hat{D}F,$

and since $\qquad\qquad A\hat{B}C = D\hat{E}F,$

$$\therefore B\hat{C}A = E\hat{F}D,$$

and in this case the triangles ABC, DEF are similar.   [Prop. 28.

(2)   If $G\hat{A}H$ be not equal to $E\hat{D}F$, draw DK, making $E\hat{D}K$ equal $B\hat{A}C$, and cutting EF at K.

Then in the triangles AGH, EDK,
$$A\hat{G}H = A\hat{B}C = D\hat{E}K,$$
$$G\hat{A}H \qquad = E\hat{D}K,$$
$$AG \qquad = DE.$$

Hence the triangles AGH, DEK are congruent.
$$\therefore AH = DK,$$
$$A\hat{H}G = D\hat{K}E.$$
But $\qquad\qquad AH = DF,$
$$\therefore DF = DK,$$
$$\therefore D\hat{K}F = D\hat{F}K.$$

Therefore $\qquad A\hat{C}B + D\hat{F}E = A\hat{H}G + D\hat{F}E$
$$= D\hat{K}E + D\hat{F}E$$
$$= D\hat{F}K + D\hat{F}E$$
$$= \text{two right angles.}$$

Art. 95.   NOTE.

Euclid's method of stating Proposition 31 amounts to the insertion of additional conditions in the statement here given, the effect of which is to exclude the second alternative in those cases in which the two alternatives are really distinct.

It is as follows :—

If two triangles have one angle of the one equal to one angle of the other, and the sides about two other angles proportionals; then if each of the remaining angles be either less or greater than a right angle, or if one of them be a right angle, the triangles are similar and have those angles equal about which the sides are proportionals.

Hence the additional conditions are that $A\hat{C}B$ and $D\hat{F}E$ are both less than a right angle, or both greater than a right angle, or one of them is a right angle.

If they are both less than a right angle, their sum is less than two right angles.

If they are both greater than a right angle, their sum is greater than two right angles.

In neither of these cases can the second alternative hold.

Hence the first alternative must hold, and the triangles are similar; the angles between the proportional sides being equal.

If next one of the two angles ACB, DFE is a right angle, then, whichever alternative hold, the other angle is a right angle, hence the remaining angles are equal, and the triangles are similar.

This is the case in which the two alternatives are not really distinct.

Art. 96.   EXAMPLE 35.

If B and C are the centres of two circles, and A the point of intersection of their internal or of their external common tangents, and if APQ be any straight line through A cutting the first circle at P and the second at Q, prove that the angles APB, AQC are either equal or supplementary.

Art. 97. PROPOSITION XXXII. (Euc. VI. 18.)

ENUNCIATION. *On a given straight line to describe a rectilineal figure similar and similarly situated to a given rectilineal figure.*

Let $A_1B_1C_1D_1E_1$ be the given rectilineal figure; it is required to describe a similar figure on the given straight line A_2B_2, so that A_1B_1 and A_2B_2 may be corresponding sides of the figures.

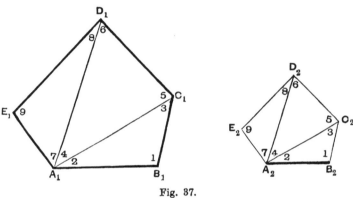

Fig. 37.

Join A_1C_1, A_1D_1.

At B_2 draw a straight line making with A_2B_2 an angle equal to $A_1\hat{B}_1C_1$, and at A_2 draw a straight line making with A_2B_2 an angle equal to $B_1A_1C_1$. Let these straight lines meet at C_2.

At C_2 draw a straight line making with A_2C_2 an angle equal to $A_1C_1D_1$, and at A_2 draw a straight line making with A_2C_2 an angle equal to $C_1A_1D_1$. Let these straight lines meet at D_2.

At D_2 draw a straight line making with D_2A_2 an angle equal to $A_1D_1E_1$, and at A_2 draw a straight line making with A_2D_2 an angle equal to $D_1A_1E_1$. Let these straight lines meet at E_2.

It will be proved that $A_1B_1C_1D_1E_1$ and $A_2B_2C_2D_2E_2$ are similar figures, and that A_1B_1 and A_2B_2 are corresponding sides.

In the three pairs of triangles in Figure 37, viz. :—$A_1B_1C_1$ and $A_2B_2C_2$, $A_1C_1D_1$ and $A_2C_2D_2$, $A_1D_1E_1$ and $A_2D_2E_2$, let the equal angles be marked with the same numbers. Then in each pair of triangles two angles of the one triangle are respectively equal to two angles in the other triangle. Therefore the remaining angles are equal. Let these be marked with the same number.

Then it is at once apparent that the angles at A_1, B_1, C_1, D_1, E_1 of the figure $A_1B_1C_1D_1E_1$ are respectively equal to the angles at A_2, B_2, C_2, D_2, E_2 of the figure $A_2B_2C_2D_2E_2$; so that the first set of conditions (see Art. 77) for the similarity of the two figures is satisfied.

Next the triangles $A_1B_1C_1$ and $A_2B_2C_2$ are equiangular and therefore by Prop. 28 are similar.

In like manner the triangles $A_1C_1D_1$ and $A_2C_2D_2$ are similar; and the triangles $A_1D_1E_1$ and $A_2D_2E_2$ are similar.

From these pairs of similar triangles follow the relations

$$B_1C_1 : B_2C_2 = C_1A_1 : C_2A_2 = A_1B_1 : A_2B_2 \dots\dots\dots\dots\dots(1),$$

$$C_1A_1 : C_2A_2 = A_1D_1 : A_2D_2 = D_1C_1 : D_2C_2 \dots\dots\dots\dots(2),$$

$$A_1D_1 : A_2D_2 = D_1E_1 : D_2E_2 = E_1A_1 : E_2A_2 \dots\dots\dots\dots\dots(3).$$

Hence

$$A_1B_1 : A_2B_2 = B_1C_1 : B_2C_2 = C_1D_1 : C_2D_2 = D_1E_1 : D_2E_2 = E_1A_1 : E_2A_2.$$

Hence the second set of conditions (see Art. 77) for the similarity of the two figures is also satisfied.

Hence the two figures $A_1B_1C_1D_1E_1$ and $A_2B_2C_2D_2E_2$ are similar figures, and A_1B_1 and A_2B_2 are corresponding sides. Therefore the figures are similarly described on A_1B_1 and A_2B_2 (see Art. 80).

Art. 98. PROPOSITION XXXIII. (Included in Euc. VI. 20.)

ENUNCIATION. *Two similar rectilineal figures may be divided into the same number of triangles such that every triangle in either figure is similar to one triangle in the other figure.*

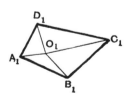 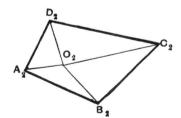

Fig. 38.

Let $A_1B_1C_1D_1$, $A_2B_2C_2D_2$ be two similar figures, such that

$$D_1\hat{A}_1B_1 = D_2\hat{A}_2B_2,$$
$$A_1\hat{B}_1C_1 = A_2\hat{B}_2C_2,$$
$$B_1\hat{C}_1D_1 = B_2\hat{C}_2D_2,$$
$$C_1\hat{D}_1A_1 = C_2\hat{D}_2A_2,$$

and $A_1B_1 : A_2B_2 = B_1C_1 : B_2C_2 = C_1D_1 : C_2D_2 = D_1A_1 : D_2A_2.$

Let O_1 be any point in the plane of $A_1B_1C_1D_1$, and join O_1A_1, O_1B_1, O_1C_1, O_1D_1.

Through A_2 draw a straight line making with A_2B_2 an angle equal to $B_1\hat{A}_1O_1$.

Through B_2 draw a straight line making with B_2A_2 an angle equal to $A_1\hat{B}_1O_1$.

Let these two straight lines meet at O_2.

Join O_2C_2, O_2D_2.

It will be proved that the triangles $O_1A_1B_1$, $O_2A_2B_2$ are similar; that the triangles $O_1B_1C_1$, $O_2B_2C_2$ are similar, and so on.

Since $O_1\hat{A}_1B_1 = O_2\hat{A}_2B_2,$

$$O_1\hat{B}_1A_1 = O_2\hat{B}_2A_2,$$
$$\therefore \ A_1\hat{O}_1B_1 = A_2\hat{O}_2B_2.$$

Hence the triangles $A_1O_1B_1$, $A_2O_2B_2$ are similar.   [Prop. 28.

$$\therefore \ A_1B_1 : A_2B_2 = B_1O_1 : B_2O_2 = O_1A_1 : O_2A_2.$$

Since $A_1B_1 : A_2B_2 = B_1C_1 : B_2C_2,$

$$\therefore \ B_1O_1 : B_2O_2 = B_1C_1 : B_2C_2,$$
$$\therefore \ B_1O_1 : B_1C_1 = B_2O_2 : B_2C_2.$$ [Prop. 24.

Also $A_1\hat{B}_1C_1 = A_2\hat{B}_2C_2;$

$$A_1\hat{B}_1O_1 = A_2\hat{B}_2O_2,$$
$$\therefore \ O_1\hat{B}_1C_1 = O_2\hat{B}_2C_2.$$

Hence by Prop. 30 the triangles $O_1B_1C_1$, $O_2B_2C_2$ are similar.

In like manner the triangles $O_1C_1D_1$ and $O_2C_2D_2$ can be proved to be similar; and also $O_1D_1A_1$, $O_2D_2A_2$ can be proved to be similar.

So the two similar figures are divided up into the same number of triangles, such that every triangle in either figure is similar to one triangle in the other figure.

The point O_1 in the one figure corresponds to the point O_2 in the other figure.

Since O_1 is any point in the one figure, it follows that to every point in one of the figures corresponds one and only one point of the other figure.

Art. 99. COROLLARY.

If in Figure 38 *the first figure be placed on the second so that O_1 falls on O_2, O_1A_1 falls along O_2A_2, O_1B_1 falls along O_2B_2, it can be shown that the sides of the first figure will then be parallel to and in the same direction as the corresponding sides of the second, and that the distances from O_1 or O_2 to a point on either figure along any straight line are in the ratio of similitude of the figures.*

If O_1 be placed on O_2, O_1A_1 along A_2O_2 produced through O_2, and O_1B_1 along B_2O_2 produced through O_2, the sides of the first figure will then be parallel but in the opposite direction to the corresponding sides of the second figure.

When the two figures have been placed as described in either of the two preceding cases, then the point O_2, with which O_1 coincides, is called a centre of similitude of the two figures.

The term centre of similitude is not however restricted to rectilineal figures. (See Art. 100, Ex. 37 below.)

Art. 100. EXAMPLES.

36. If two similar rectilineal figures are placed so that two consecutive sides of one figure are respectively parallel and both in the same direction as, or both in the opposite direction to, the corresponding sides of the other figure, then each side of the one figure will be parallel to the corresponding side of the other figure, and the straight lines joining corresponding angular points of the two figures are all parallel or meet in a point; and in the latter case the distances from that point along any straight line to the points where it meets corresponding sides of the figures are in the ratio of similitude of the figures.

What is the ratio of similitude when the lines joining corresponding angular points are parallel?

37. If the straight line joining the centres A, B of two circles be divided internally and externally in the ratio of the radii of the circles, (the segment of the line AB terminated at A corresponding to the radius of the circle whose centre is A), then show that the points of division may be regarded as centres of similitude of the circles.

Art. 101. PROPOSITION XXXIV. (Euc. VI. 8.)

ENUNCIATION. *If a right-angled triangle be divided into two parts by a perpendicular drawn from the vertex of the right angle on to the hypotenuse, then the triangles so formed are similar to each other and to the whole triangle; the perpendicular is a mean proportional between the segments of the hypotenuse; and each side is a mean proportional between the adjacent segment of the hypotenuse and the hypotenuse.*

If ABC be the triangle, and B the vertex of the right angle, and if BD be drawn perpendicular to AC, it is required to prove

(1)   that the triangles ABC, ABD, BDC are similar.

(2)   that BD is a mean proportional between AD and DC.

(3)   that BC is a mean proportional between CD and AC.

(4)   that BA is a mean proportional between AD and AC.

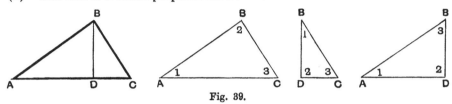

Fig. 39.

The triangles ABC, ABD will be compared first.

$$B\hat{A}C = B\hat{A}D$$
$$A\hat{B}C = A\hat{D}B = \text{a right angle.}$$
$$\therefore \ A\hat{C}B = A\hat{B}D.$$

Hence the triangles are similar (Prop. 28).

$$\therefore \ BC : DB = CA : BA = AB : AD.$$

Since $\qquad\qquad CA : BA = BA : AD,$

$\therefore BA$ is a mean proportional between AC and AD.

In like manner it can be shown that the triangles ABC, DBC are similar; and that BC is a mean proportional between AC and CD.

Since ABD, CBD are similar to ABC they are similar to one another.

$$B\hat{A}D = D\hat{B}C$$
$$A\hat{B}D = B\hat{C}D$$
$$A\hat{D}B = B\hat{D}C,$$
$$\therefore \ DB : DC = BA : CB = AD : BD.$$

Hence $\qquad\qquad DB : DC = AD : DB,$

$$\therefore \ DC : DB = DB : DA. \qquad\qquad \text{[Prop. 21.}$$

Hence DB is a mean proportional between DA and DC.

Art. 102.   EXAMPLE 38.

If in any triangle ABC, BD is drawn to cut AC at D so that $B\hat{D}C$ is equal to $A\hat{B}C$, prove that the triangles ABC, BCD are similar; that BC is a mean proportional between AC and CD, and that $AC : AB = BC : BD$.

SECTION VI.

Art. 103. PROPOSITION XXXV. (Euc. VI. 13.)

ENUNCIATION. *To find a mean proportional between two given segments of straight lines.*

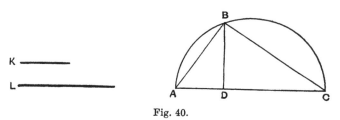

Fig. 40.

Let the given straight lines be K and L.

Take a straight line AD equal to K, and produce AD to C, so that DC is equal to L.

On AC as diameter describe a semicircle.

Through D draw DB perpendicular to AC to cut the semicircle at B.

Then DB is the mean proportional between K and L required.

Join AB, BC.

Then ABC being the angle in a semicircle is a right angle.

Also BD, being drawn perpendicular to AC from the vertex B of the right angle, is by Prop. 34 part (2) a mean proportional between AD and DC.

$\therefore$ BD is a mean proportional between K and L.

Art. 104. EXAMPLES.

39. Solve the problem of the last proposition by means of Proposition 34 (3) or (4).

40. If two circles touch each other and also touch a given straight line, prove that the part of the straight line between the points of contact is a mean proportional between the diameters of the circles.

41. If through the middle point A of the arc BAC of a circle, a chord be drawn cutting the chord of the arc BC at D and the circle again at E, prove that AB is a mean proportional between AD and AE.

42. If C be the centre of a circle, O a point outside it, OT a tangent from O to the circle, TP a perpendicular from T on OC, then prove that the radius of the circle is a mean proportional between CO and CP.

Art. 105. PROPOSITION XXXVI. (i). (Euc. VI. 3 and A, 1st Part.)

ENUNCIATION. *If the interior or exterior vertical angle of a triangle be bisected by a straight line which also cuts the base, the base is divided internally or externally in the ratio of the sides of the triangle.*

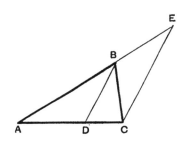

Fig. 41.

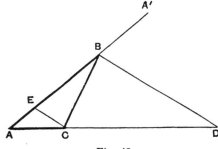

Fig. 42.

Let ABC be a triangle.

Let BD bisect the interior angle ABC in Fig. 41, but the exterior angle $A'BC$ between CB and AB produced to A' in Fig. 42.

Let BD cut the base at D.

To prove that $AD : DC = AB : BC$.

Draw CE parallel to BD cutting AB at E.

Then $\qquad\qquad B\hat{E}C = D\hat{B}A$ in Fig. 41 (or $D\hat{B}A'$ in Fig. 42)

$$= D\hat{B}C$$

$$= B\hat{C}E,$$

$$\therefore\ B\hat{E}C = B\hat{C}E,$$

$$\therefore\ BC = BE.$$

Since ADC, ABE are cut by parallel lines BD, CE,

$$\therefore\ AD : DC = AB : BE, \qquad\qquad \text{[Prop. 17.}$$

$$\therefore\ AD : DC = AB : BC.$$

Art. 106. PROPOSITION XXXVI. (ii). (Euc. VI. 3 and A, 2nd Part.)

ENUNCIATION. *If the base of a triangle be divided internally or externally in the ratio of the sides of the triangle, the straight line drawn from the point of division to the vertex bisects the interior or exterior vertical angle.*

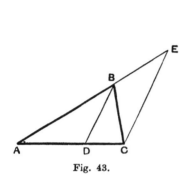

Fig. 43.

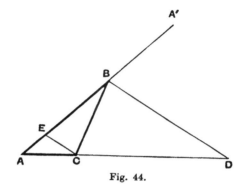

Fig. 44.

Let ABC be a triangle.

Let D divide the base AC, internally in Fig. 43, externally in Fig. 44, so that
$$AD : DC = AB : BC.$$

To prove that DB bisects the interior angle ABC in Fig. 43, but the exterior angle between CB and AB produced through B in Fig. 44.

Join DB, and draw CE parallel to DB cutting AB at E.

Then $\qquad\qquad AD : DC = AB : BE,$ $\qquad\qquad$ [Prop. 17.

but $\qquad\qquad\quad AD : DC = AB : BC,$

$\therefore\quad AB : BE = AB : BC,$

$\therefore\quad BE = BC,$ $\qquad\qquad$ [Prop. 23.

$\therefore\quad B\hat{C}E = B\hat{E}C.$

Now $A\hat{B}D$ in Fig. 43, or $A'\hat{B}D$ in Fig. 44 $= B\hat{E}C$

$= B\hat{C}E$

$= D\hat{B}C,$

$\therefore\ A\hat{B}D$ in Fig. 43, or $A'\hat{B}D$ in Fig. 44 $= D\hat{B}C.$

Hence DB bisects the interior vertical angle in Fig. 43, but the exterior vertical angle in Fig. 44.

Art. 107. EXAMPLES.

43. If the internal and external angles at B of the triangle ABC be bisected by straight lines which cut the side AC at D and E respectively, show that A, D, C, E are four harmonic points.

44. By means of Proposition 36 construct the fourth harmonic to three given points A, B, C on a straight line; considering separately the cases which arise according as the fourth harmonic is to be conjugate to A or B or C.

45. If ABC be a triangle inscribed in a circle, PQ a diameter of the circle perpendicular to AC, if CB cut PQ at R, and AB cut PQ at S, prove that

$$QR : RP = QS : SP.$$

Hence construct the fourth harmonic to three given points on a straight line.

46. Divide a given arc of a circle into two parts so that the chords of these parts may be to each other in a given ratio.

47. A point P moves in a plane so that the ratio of its distances from two fixed points A, B in that plane is always the same. Show that *in general* the locus of P is a circle, the extremities of one diameter of which are the points dividing AB internally and externally in the given ratio. What is the exceptional case?

48. The side BC of a triangle ABC is bisected at D, and the angles ADC, ADB are bisected by the straight lines DE, DF meeting AC, AB at E, F respectively. Prove that EF is parallel to BC.

49. If the bisector of the angle A of the triangle ABC cut BC at D, and if the bisector of the angle B cut AC at E, and if DE be parallel to AB, prove that the triangle ABC is isosceles.

50. If ABC be a triangle, if D be the middle point of BC, if any straight line through D cut AB at E, AC at F, and a parallel through A to BC at G; then prove that E, D, F, G are four harmonic points.

Hence show that if any point O be joined to four harmonic points, they will be cut by any transversal in four harmonic points.

Art. 108. *Def.* 14. HARMONIC LINES.

If four concurrent straight lines be cut by any transversal in four harmonic points they are called four harmonic lines, or are said to form a harmonic pencil.

SECTION VII.

AN IMPORTANT PROPOSITION IN THE THEORY OF RATIO.

Art. 109. PROPOSITION XXXVII.

If A, B, C are three magnitudes of the same kind;
if T, U, V are three magnitudes of the same kind;
if $A : B = T : U$
and $B : C = U : V$,
then will $A : C = T : V$.

Compare $A : C$ with any rational fraction $\dfrac{s}{r}$.

By Art. 48 it is necessary to consider only the two cases

$$(1) \qquad A : C > \frac{s}{r}.$$

$$(2) \qquad A : C < \frac{s}{r}.$$

In case (1) $A : C > \dfrac{s}{r}$,

$$rA > sC. \hspace{3cm} \text{[Prop. 13.}$$

Hence $rA - sC$ is a magnitude of the same kind as B.

Hence by Archimedes' Axiom (Art. 22) an integer n exists, such that

$$n (rA - sC) > B,$$
$$\therefore\ nrA > nsC + B.$$

Hence a multiple of B, say tB, exists, such that   [Prop. 8.

$$nrA > tB > nsC.$$

Since $nrA > tB$,

$$\therefore\ A : B > \frac{t}{nr}. \hspace{2.5cm} \text{[Prop. 13.}$$

But $$A : B = T : U,$$

$$\therefore \ T : U > \frac{t}{nr},$$

$$\therefore \ nrT > tU. \qquad \text{[Prop. 13.}$$

Since $$tB > nsC,$$

$$\therefore \ B : C > \frac{ns}{t}. \qquad \text{[Prop. 13.}$$

But $$B : C = U : V,$$

$$\therefore \ U : V > \frac{ns}{t},$$

$$\therefore \ tU > nsV. \qquad \text{[Prop. 13.}$$

But $$nrT > tU,$$

$$\therefore \ nrT > nsV,$$

$$\therefore \ rT > sV,$$

$$\therefore \ T : V > \frac{s}{r}. \qquad \text{[Prop. 13.}$$

In case (2) $$A : C < \frac{s}{r},$$

$$\therefore \ rA < sC. \qquad \text{[Prop 13.}$$

Hence $sC - rA$ is a magnitude of the same kind as B.

Hence by Archimedes' Axiom an integer n exists, such that

$$n \, (sC - rA) > B,$$

$$\therefore \ nsC > nrA + B.$$

Hence a multiple of B exists, say tB, such that   [Prop. 8.

$$nrA < tB < nsC.$$

Since $$nrA < tB,$$

$$\therefore \ A : B < \frac{t}{nr}. \qquad \text{[Prop. 13.}$$

But $$A : B = T : U,$$

$$\therefore \ T : U < \frac{t}{nr},$$

$$\therefore \ nrT < tU. \qquad \text{[Prop. 13.}$$

Since $$tB < nsC,$$

$$\therefore \ B : C < \frac{ns}{t}. \qquad \text{[Prop. 13.}$$

But
$$B : C = U : V,$$

$$\therefore\ U : V < \frac{ns}{t},$$

$$\therefore\ tU < ns\,V. \qquad \text{[Prop. 13.}$$

But
$$nrT < tU,$$

$$\therefore\ nrT < ns\,V,$$

$$\therefore\ rT < s\,V,$$

$$\therefore\ T : V < \frac{s}{r}. \qquad \text{[Prop. 13.}$$

It has therefore been proved

(1)   If $A : C > \dfrac{s}{r}$, then $T : V > \dfrac{s}{r}$.

(2)   If $A : C < \dfrac{s}{r}$, then $T : V < \dfrac{s}{r}$.

Hence by Art. 48
$$A : C = T : V.$$

Art. 110.   EXAMPLE 51.

Two circles whose centres are C and C' intercept equal chords AB and $A'B'$ on a straight line cutting both circles.

The tangents at A and A' meet at T.

Prove that
$$AT : A'T = AC : A'C'.$$

SECTION VIII.

AREAS.

PROPOSITIONS 38—50.

Art. 111. PROPOSITION XXXVIII (i). (**Euc. VI. 16, 1st Part.**)

ENUNCIATION. *If four straight lines are proportional, the rectangle contained by the extremes is equal to the rectangle contained by the means.*

Let K, L, M, P be the straight lines, such that

$$K : L = M : P,$$

it is required to prove that the rectangle contained by K and P is equal to that contained by L and M.

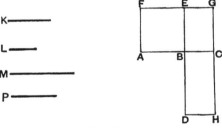

Fig. 45.

Take AB equal to K.

Produce AB to C so that BC is equal to L.

Through B draw BD equal to M perpendicular to AB, and produce DB to E so that BE is equal to P.

Complete the rectangles $ABEF$, $BCGE$, $BCHD$.

Since rectangles having equal altitudes are proportional to their bases (Prop. 16)

$$ABEF : BCGE = AB : BC = K : L,$$
$$BCHD : BCGE = BD : BE = M : P.$$

Now $K : L = M : P,$

$\therefore ABEF : BCGE = BCHD : BCGE,$

$\therefore ABEF = BCHD.$ [Art. 43.

Now $ABEF$ is the rectangle contained by AB and BE, i.e. by K and P.

Whilst $BCHD$ is the rectangle contained by BC and BD, i.e. by L and M.

$\therefore$ the rectangle contained by K and P is equal to that contained by L and M.

Art. 112.   PROPOSITION XXXVIII (ii).   (Euc. VI. 16, 2nd Part.)

ENUNCIATION. *Let there be four straight lines, which taken in a definite order are K, L, M, P; and let it be given that the rectangle contained by the first and fourth, K and P, is equal to the rectangle contained by the second and third, L and M; to prove that*

$$K : L = M : P.$$

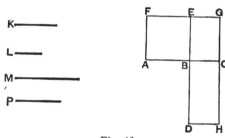

Fig. 46.

Make the same construction as in the preceding part of the proposition.

The rectangle contained by K and P is the rectangle contained by AB and BE and is therefore $ABEF$.

The rectangle contained by L and M is the rectangle contained by BC and BD, and is therefore $BCHD$.

$\therefore ABEF$ is given equal to $BCHD$.

$\therefore ABEF : BCGE = BCHD : BCGE,$ [Art. 43.

but $ABEF : BCGE = AB : BC = K : L,$ [Prop. 16.

and $BCHD : BCGE = BD : BE = M : P,$ [Prop. 16.

$\therefore K : L = M : P.$

11—2

Art. 113. COROLLARY TO PROPOSITION 38. (Euc. VI. 17.)

PART 1. *If three straight lines are proportionals, the rectangle contained by the extremes is equal to the square on the mean.*

PART 2. *Let there be three straight lines, which taken in a definite order are K, L, and P; and let it be given that the rectangle contained by the first and third, K and P, is equal to the square on the second, L, then it will follow that*

$$K : L = L : P.$$

The first part is the particular case of Proposition 38 (i), and the second part the particular case of Proposition 38 (ii), when $M = L$.

Art. 114. EXAMPLES.

52. Let C be the centre of a circle, O any point in its plane; let A and B be the extremities of the diameter through O; let P and Q be the extremities of any chord through O. Prove that the circle drawn through C, P and Q cuts OC in a point D which is the same for all directions of the chord OPQ, and show that

$$OA : OD = OC : OB.$$

53. (i) Let A be the centre of a circle, B a point outside it, BD and BE tangents to the circle, C the point in which DE cuts AB, BFG a straight line through B cutting the circle at F and G; then prove that the rectangle $BA \cdot BC$ is equal to the rectangle $BF \cdot BG$. Prove that CD bisects the angle FCG, and that if CD cut FG at H, then B, F, H, G are four harmonic points.

(ii) Let A be the centre of a circle, B a point inside the circle, and let any chord GBF be drawn through B, and produced to H so that G, B, F, H are four harmonic points, prove that the locus of H is a straight line which cuts AB at right angles at a point C such that the rectangle $BA \cdot BC$ is equal to the rectangle $BF \cdot BG$.

54. If A, B, C, D are four harmonic points and O the middle point between the two conjugate points A and C, prove that the rectangle contained by OB and OD is equal to the square on OC.

Art. 115. *Def.* 15. POLE AND POLAR.

If through any point O a straight line be drawn cutting a circle at P and Q, and on OPQ a point R be taken so that O, P, R, Q are four harmonic points, O and R being conjugates; then the locus of R is called the polar line of O, and O is called the pole of the locus of R.

It is a result of Example 53 that the polar line is a straight line.

Art. 116.   EXAMPLES.

55.   If C be the centre of a circle, O any point in its plane and T the foot of the perpendicular from C on to the polar line of O, then prove that the rectangle contained by CO and CT is equal to the square on the radius of the circle.

56.   If A lie on the polar of B with regard to a circle, show that B lies on the polar of A with regard to that circle.

(Two such points as A, B are said to be conjugate with regard to the circle.)

57.   If two circles cut at right angles prove that the extremities of any diameter of either circle are conjugate points with regard to the other circle.

58.   If A, B be two points, and if from A a perpendicular AP be drawn to the polar line of B with regard to a circle whose centre is C, and if from B a perpendicular BQ be drawn to the polar line of A, prove that

$$CA : CB = AP : BQ,$$

and show that the triangles CAP, CBQ are similar.

59.   Let C be the centre of a circle, V any fixed point in its plane, let CV cut the circumference at A, and let a point P be taken on CV so that the rectangle $CV . CP$ is equal to the square on CA.   Let a straight line PY be drawn through P perpendicular to CP, and let PY be cut by any straight line through V in W, and by a perpendicular through C to VW in X, prove that the rectangle $PX . PW$ will always be equal to the rectangle $CP . PV$ in whatever direction the straight line VW may be drawn.

Art. 117.   *Def.* 16.   INVERSE LOCUS.   CENTRE OF INVERSION.

If from any point O a straight line be drawn to cut any curve at P, and on OP a point Q be taken so that the rectangle $OP . OQ$ has a constant area, then the locus of Q is called the inverse of the locus of P with regard to O as centre (or origin) of inversion.

The side of the square whose area is equal to the constant rectangle $OP . OQ$ is called the radius of inversion.

Also P and Q are said to be inverse points with regard to the circle whose centre is O, and whose radius is the radius of inversion.

Art. 118.   EXAMPLES.

60.   If the locus of P is a circle, show that the inverse locus is generally a circle, but will be a straight line if the centre of inversion be a point on the circle on which P lies.

61. If the locus of P is a straight line show that the inverse locus is a circle passing through the centre of inversion.

62. If two circles or a straight line and a circle or two straight lines intersect one another, show that their angle of intersection is equal to the angle of intersection of their inverse loci.

Art. 119. *Def.* 17. THE RADICAL AXIS OF TWO CIRCLES.

The locus of points from which tangents drawn to two circles are of equal length is called the radical axis of the two circles.

Art. 120. EXAMPLES.

63. If two circles intersect, show that the straight line joining their points of intersection is their radical axis.

If they do not intersect, show that the radical axis is perpendicular to the line joining the centres of the circles, and cuts it at a point which is such that double the distance of this point from the point half way between the centres of the circles is a fourth proportional to the distance between the centres of the circles, the sum of their radii and the difference of their radii.

64. Show that the difference between the squares of the tangents from any point P to two circles is equal to twice the rectangle contained by the perpendicular from P on the radical axis, and the distance between the centres of the circles.

65. Show how to choose the centre and the radius of inversion so that two given circles may be inverted each into itself.

Art. 121. PROPOSITION XXXIX.

ENUNCIATION. *The rectangle contained by the diagonals of a quadrilateral cannot be greater than the sum of the rectangles contained by opposite sides.* (It may be equal, and in that case a circle can be described through the vertices of the quadrilateral.)

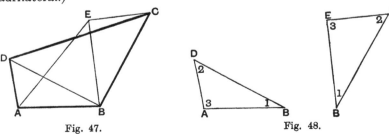

Fig. 47.   Fig. 48.

Let $ABCD$ be a quadrilateral.

It is required to prove that the rectangle $AC.BD$ cannot be greater than the sum of the rectangles $AD.BC$ and $AB.CD$.

On BC describe the triangle BCE similar to ABD, so that the side BC of BCE may correspond to the side BD of ABD.

Then
$$C\hat{B}E = A\hat{B}D,$$
$$B\hat{C}E = B\hat{D}A,$$
$$B\hat{E}C = B\hat{A}D.$$

Also $BD : BC = DA : CE = AB : EB.$

From the first and second ratios it follows by Prop. 38 (i) that
$$\text{rect. } BD.CE = \text{rect. } AD.BC.$$

Also from the first and third ratios
$$BD : BC = BA : BE,$$
but also
$$D\hat{B}C = D\hat{B}E + E\hat{B}C$$
$$= D\hat{B}E + D\hat{B}A$$
$$= A\hat{B}E.$$

Hence by Prop. 30 the triangles DBC, ABE are similar.

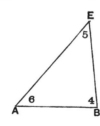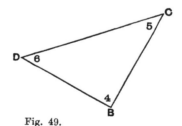

Fig. 49.

The side BD corresponds to BA,

the side BC corresponds to BE,

and the side CD corresponds to AE.

$$\therefore \quad BD : BA = DC : AE = CB : EB.$$

From the first and second ratios by Prop. 38 (i)
$$\text{rect. } BD.AE = \text{rect. } AB.CD.$$

Now it has been shown that
$$\text{rect. } BD.CE = \text{rect. } AD.BC,$$
$$\therefore \text{ rect. } BD.AE + \text{rect. } BD.CE = \text{rect. } AB.CD + \text{rect. } AD.BC.$$

Now AC cannot be greater than $AE + EC$.

(The case in which AC is equal to $AE + EC$ will be considered below.)

∴ rect. $BD . AC$ cannot be greater than rect. $BD . AE$ + rect. $BD . CE$.

∴ rect. $BD . AC$ cannot be greater than rect. $AB . CD$ + rect. $AD . BC$.

If $AC = AE + EC$,

then E lies on AC,

and   rect. $BD . AC$ = rect. $AB . CD$ + rect. $AD . BC$.

Now $B\hat{C}E = B\hat{D}A$,

whilst in this case $B\hat{C}E = B\hat{C}A$.

∴ $B\hat{C}A = B\hat{D}A$,

and therefore the circle circumscribing ABD passes through C.

Hence a circle can be described about the vertices of the quadrilateral $ABCD$.

Art. 122. It is interesting to examine what happens when D and C are points on the straight line AB.

In this case the straight line can be regarded as a circle of infinite radius.

Hence taking the points on the line in the order A, B, C, D the lines corresponding to the diagonals are AC, BD; whilst AB, CD correspond to one pair of opposite sides; and BC, AD to the other pair.

Hence   rect. $AC . BD$ = rect. $AB . CD$ + rect. $BC . AD$.

This result is easily verified.

Art. 123. PROPOSITION XL. (Euc. VI. 23.)

ENUNCIATION. *To construct two straight lines whose ratio is equal to the ratio of the areas of two equiangular parallelograms.*

Since the parallelograms are equiangular they may be placed so as to have a common angle, and their sides along the same straight lines, but in opposite directions.

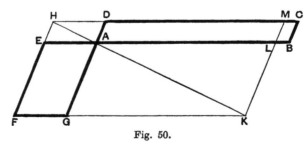

Fig. 50.

When this has been done let $ABCD$ be one parallelogram, let $AEFG$ be the other.

Produce MD and FE to meet at H.

Join HA.

Produce HA to meet FG at K.

Draw KLM parallel to AD to meet AB, DC at L, M respectively.

Then $AEFG$ is equal to $ALMD$, since they are complements about the diameter of a parallelogram.

$$\therefore\ ABCD : AEFG = ABCD : ALMD \qquad \text{[Prop. 22.}$$
$$= AB : AL. \qquad \text{[Prop. 16.}$$

The two lines required are therefore AB and AL.

In this way the problem of finding the ratio of two areas is reduced to the simpler one of finding the ratio of two lengths.

The close connection of the construction employed in this proposition with that given by Euclid in the 44th proposition of the First Book should be noted.

Art. 124. It is worth while to notice the relation of the line AL to the sides of the parallelograms $ABCD$, $AEFG$.

$AB : AE$ is the ratio of one side of the first parallelogram to one side of the second parallelogram.

$AD : AG$ is the ratio of the other side of the first parallelogram to the other side of the second parallelogram.

But since the triangles ADH, AGK are equiangular, they are similar, and therefore

$$AD : AG = DH : GK = HA : KA.$$

Now $$DH = AE,$$

and $$GK = AL.$$

Hence $$AD : AG = AE : AL.$$

Hence the two ratios of the sides of the parallelograms are $AB : AE$, and $AD : AG$ which is equal to $AE : AL$.

And the ratio of the areas of the parallelograms is $AB : AL$.

Art. 125. PROPOSITION XLI.

ENUNCIATION. *The ratio of the areas of two equiangular parallelograms is equal to the ratio of the areas of the rectangles contained by their sides.*

This follows immediately from the preceding proposition by observing that the ratio $AB:AL$ depends only on the lengths of the sides, and not at all on the common angle of the parallelograms.

For AL is determined by the proportion $AD:AG=AE:AL$.

Hence if a rectangle be constructed whose sides are equal to AB, AD and another rectangle constructed whose sides are equal to AE, AG; the ratio of the first rectangle to the second will as before be equal to $AB:AL$, and therefore equal to the ratio of the parallelogram $ABCD$ to the parallelogram $AEFG$.

Art. 126. PROPOSITION XLII.

ENUNCIATION. *If three straight lines be in proportion, then the ratio of the area of the square described on the first line to the area of the square described on the second line is equal to the ratio of the first line to the third line.*

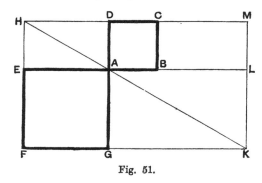

Fig. 51.

Let $ABCD$, $AEFG$ be two squares placed so that they have a common vertex and their sides on the same straight lines but in opposite directions.

Constructing the figure with the same letters as in Prop. 40, then

$$\text{area } ABCD:\text{area } AEFG = AB:AL,$$

where as before $$AD:AG=AE:AL.$$

But $$AD = AB,$$
and $$AG = AE,$$
$$\therefore \ AB : AE = AE : AL.$$

Hence   the square described on AB : the square described on AE
$$= AB : AL,$$
where AL is determined by the proportion
$$AB : AE = AE : AL.$$

This result will be repeatedly required in what follows, and should be carefully remembered.

Art. 127. PROPOSITION XLIII. (Euc. VI. 19.)

ENUNCIATION. *The ratio of the areas of two similar triangles is equal to the ratio of the areas of the squares described on corresponding sides*.*

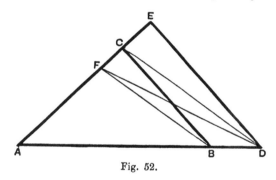

Fig. 52.

The triangles being similar may be placed so as to have a common vertex, and the corresponding sides which meet at this vertex along the same straight lines and in the same direction.

When this is done, let the triangles be ABC and ADE.

Since $$A\hat{B}C = A\hat{D}E,$$
$$\therefore \ BC \text{ is parallel to } DE.$$

Join DC.

Draw BF parallel to DC to cut AE at F.

Join DF.

* On account of the importance of this proposition an independent proof is given. See Note 10.

Since BF and DC are parallel,

$$\therefore \triangle BCF = \triangle BDF.$$

Add to each $\triangle ABF$,

$$\therefore \triangle ABF + \triangle BFC = \triangle ABF + \triangle BDF,$$

$$\therefore \triangle ABC = \triangle ADF,$$

$$\therefore \triangle ADE : \triangle ABC = \triangle ADE : \triangle ADF \qquad \text{[Prop. 22.}$$

$$= AE : AF. \qquad \text{[Prop. 16.}$$

But $\qquad AE : AC = AD : AB$

since the triangles ADE, ABC are similar.

And $\qquad AD : AB = AC : AF$

since DC is parallel to BF.

$$\therefore AE : AC = AC : AF.$$

Hence by Prop. 42

$\qquad$ square described on AE : square described on AC

$$= AE : AF$$

$$= \triangle ADE : \triangle ABC.$$

Now AE and AC are corresponding sides of the triangles ADE, ABC.

Consequently the ratio of the areas of two similar triangles is equal to the ratio of the areas of the squares described on corresponding sides.

Art. 128.   EXAMPLE 66.

If ABC be a triangle, and if BE, CF be drawn perpendicular to the sides AC, AB respectively; prove that the triangle ABE is to the triangle ACF as the square on AB is to the square on AC.

Art. 129.   PROPOSITION XLIV. (i).

ENUNCIATION. *If four straight lines are proportional, then the squares described on them are proportional.*

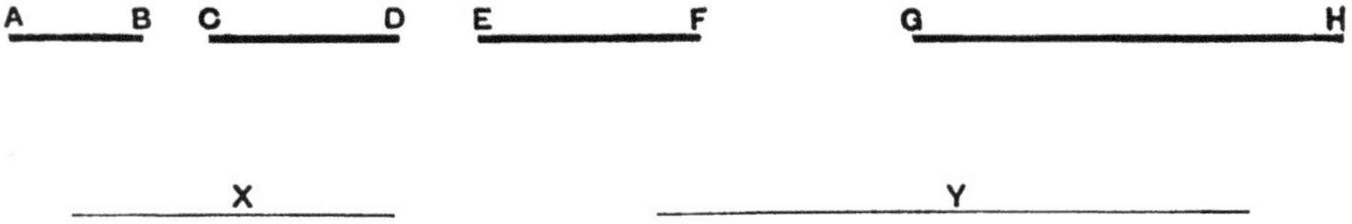

Fig. 53.

Let AB, CD, EF, GH be four straight lines such that
$$AB : CD = EF : GH. \qquad (1)$$
It is required to prove that
$$\text{sq. on } AB : \text{sq. on } CD = \text{sq. on } EF : \text{sq. on } GH.$$
Construct straight lines X and Y such that
$$AB : CD = CD : X, \qquad (2)$$
$$EF : GH = GH : Y. \qquad (3)$$
It follows from (1), (2), (3) that
$$CD : X = GH : Y. \qquad (4)$$
From (1) and (4) by Prop. 37 it follows that
$$AB : X = EF : Y,$$
but
$$AB : X = \text{sq. on } AB : \text{sq. on } CD \qquad \text{[Prop. 42.}$$
and
$$EF : Y = \text{sq. on } EF : \text{sq. on } GH, \qquad \text{[Prop. 42.}$$
$$\therefore \text{ sq. on } AB : \text{sq. on } CD = \text{sq. on } EF : \text{sq. on } GH.$$

Art. 130.   PROPOSITION XLIV. (ii).

ENUNCIATION. *If four squares are in proportion, their sides will be in proportion.*

Let AB, CD, EF, GH be four lines such that
$$\text{sq. on } AB : \text{sq. on } CD = \text{sq. on } EF : \text{sq. on } GH.$$
Take a line X such that
$$AB : CD = EF : X.$$
Then it has been shown that
$$\text{sq. on } AB : \text{sq. on } CD = \text{sq. on } EF : \text{sq. on } X, \qquad \text{[Prop. 44 (i).}$$
$$\therefore \text{ sq. on } EF : \text{sq. on } GH = \text{sq. on } EF : \text{sq. on } X,$$
$$\therefore \text{ sq. on } GH = \text{sq. on } X, \qquad \text{[Prop. 23.}$$
$$\therefore GH = X.$$
$$\therefore AB : CD = EF : GH.$$

Art. 131.   PROPOSITION XLV.   (Euc. V. 12.)

ENUNCIATION. *If there be any number of equal ratios in which the magnitudes are all of the same kind, then the ratio of any antecedent to its consequent is equal to the ratio of the sum of the antecedents to the sum of the consequents ; i.e. if*
$$A : B = C : D = E : F,$$
then
$$A : B = A + C + E : B + D + F.$$

Compare $A : B$ with the ratio $\dfrac{s}{r}$.

There are three possible alternatives,

$$(1) \quad A : B > \frac{s}{r},$$

$$(2) \quad A : B = \frac{s}{r},$$

$$(3) \quad A : B < \frac{s}{r}.$$

Of these it is not necessary to consider the second.   [Art. 48.

In case (1) $A : B > \dfrac{s}{r},$

$$\therefore \; rA > sB. \qquad\qquad\qquad \text{[Prop. 13.}$$

Since $A : B = C : D = E : F,$

$$\therefore \; C : D > \frac{s}{r},$$

$$\therefore \; rC > sD, \qquad\qquad\qquad \text{[Prop. 13.}$$

and $E : F > \dfrac{s}{r},$

$$\therefore \; rE > sF, \qquad\qquad\qquad \text{[Prop. 13.}$$

but also $rA > sB,$

$$\therefore \; rA + rC + rE > sB + sD + sF,$$

$$\therefore \; r(A + C + E) > s(B + D + F),$$

$$\therefore \; A + C + E : B + D + F > \frac{s}{r}. \qquad \text{[Prop. 13.}$$

Hence if $A : B > \dfrac{s}{r},$

then $A + C + E : B + D + F > \dfrac{s}{r}.$

*In like manner it can be shown that in case (3) if

$$A : B < \frac{s}{r},$$

then $A + C + E : B + D + F < \dfrac{s}{r}.$

$$\therefore \; A : B = A + C + E : B + D + F. \qquad \text{[Art. 48.}$$

---

* The demonstration of case (3) can be deduced from that of case (1) by replacing the sign $>$ by the sign $<$ throughout.

Art. 132.   EXAMPLE 67.

The perimeters of similar triangles (or similar rectilineal figures) are to one another in the ratio of corresponding sides.

Art. 133.   PROPOSITION XLVI.   (Euc. VI. 20.)

ENUNCIATION.   *The ratio of the areas of two similar rectilineal figures is equal to the ratio of the areas of the squares described on corresponding sides.*

Let $A_1B_1C_1D_1$ and $A_2B_2C_2D_2$ be similar figures, and A_1B_1, A_2B_2 corresponding sides.

To prove that

$$A_1B_1C_1D_1 : A_2B_2C_2D_2 = \text{square on } A_1B_1 : \text{square on } A_2B_2.$$

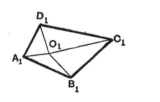 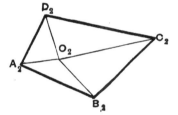

Fig. 54.

Taking the figure of Proposition 33 it was proved that the triangles $O_1A_1B_1$, $O_2A_2B_2$ were similar, as were also $O_1B_1C_1$ and $O_2B_2C_2$, $O_1C_1D_1$ and $O_2C_2D_2$, $O_1D_1A_1$ and $O_2D_2A_2$.

Hence by Prop. 43

$$\triangle O_1A_1B_1 : \triangle O_2A_2B_2 = \text{square on } A_1B_1 : \text{square on } A_2B_2,$$

$$\triangle O_1B_1C_1 : \triangle O_2B_2C_2 = \text{square on } B_1C_1 : \text{square on } B_2C_2,$$

$$\triangle O_1C_1D_1 : \triangle O_2C_2D_2 = \text{square on } C_1D_1 : \text{square on } C_2D_2,$$

$$\triangle O_1D_1A_1 : \triangle O_2D_2A_2 = \text{square on } D_1A_1 : \text{square on } D_2A_2.$$

But since the figures are similar

$$A_1B_1 : A_2B_2 = B_1C_1 : B_2C_2 = C_1D_1 : C_2D_2 = D_1A_1 : D_2A_2.$$

Hence by Prop. 44 the ratios of the squares described on these lines are equal.

$$\therefore \ \triangle O_1A_1B_1 : \triangle O_2A_2B_2 = \triangle O_1B_1C_1 : \triangle O_2B_2C_2 = \triangle O_1C_1D_1 : \triangle O_2C_2D_2 = \triangle O_1D_1A_1 : \triangle O_2D_2A_2.$$

Hence by Prop. 45

$$\triangle O_1 A_1 B_1 : \triangle O_2 A_2 B_2$$

$$= \triangle O_1 A_1 B_1 + \triangle O_1 B_1 C_1 + \triangle O_1 C_1 D_1 + \triangle O_1 D_1 A_1 : \triangle O_2 A_2 B_2 + \triangle O_2 B_2 C_2 + \triangle O_2 C_2 D_2 + \triangle O_2 D_2 A_2$$

$$= \text{figure } A_1 B_1 C_1 D_1 : \text{figure } A_2 B_2 C_2 D_2.$$

∴ figure $A_1 B_1 C_1 D_1$: figure $A_2 B_2 C_2 D_2$ = square on $A_1 B_1$: square on $A_2 B_2$.

Art. 134. PROPOSITION XLVII. (i). (Euc. VI. 22, 1st Part.)

ENUNCIATION. *Let there be four straight lines A, B, C, D which are in proportion.*

Let two similar rectilinear figures be similarly described on A and B.

Let two similar rectilinear figures be similarly described on C and D.

It is required to prove that

  the area of the figure on A : the area of the figure on B

  = the area of the figure on C : the area of the figure on D.

Let the areas of the similar figures similarly described on A and B be U and V respectively.

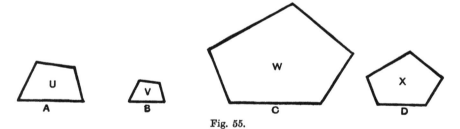

Fig. 55.

Then $U : V =$ square on A : square on B.   [Prop. 46.

Let the areas of the similar figures similarly described on C and D be W and X respectively.

Then $W : X =$ square on C : square on D.   [Prop. 46.

Now $A : B = C : D,$

  ∴ the square on A : the square on B

  = the square on C : the square on D.   [Prop. 44 (i).

        ∴ $U : V = W : X.$

Art. 135. PROPOSITION XLVII. (ii). (Euc. VI. 22, 2nd Part.)

ENUNCIATION. *Let there be four straight lines A, B, C, D.*

Let two similar figures be similarly described on A and B.

Let two similar figures be similarly described on C and D.

Let it be given that

> *the area of the figure on A : the area of the figure on B*
>
> *= the area of the figure on C : the area of the figure on D.*

It is required to prove that

$$A : B = C : D.$$

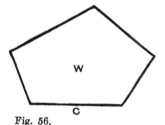

Fig. 56.

Let the areas of the similar figures on A and B be U and V respectively.

Then $U : V =$ the square on A : the square on B.   [Prop. 46.

Let the areas of the similar figures on C and D be W and X respectively.

Then $W : X =$ the square on C : the square on D.   [Prop. 46.

It is given that $U : V = W : X,$

$\therefore$ the square on A : the square on B

$=$ the square on C : the square on D.

$\therefore A : B = C : D.$ [Prop. 44 (ii).

Art. 136. PROPOSITION XLVIII. (Euc. VI. 31.)*

ENUNCIATION. *In any right-angled triangle, any rectilineal figure described on the hypotenuse is equal to the sum of the two similar and similarly described figures on the sides.*

Let ABC be a triangle right-angled at C.

On AB let any rectilineal figure Z be described.

---

* I am indebted to Mr H. M. Taylor, the author of the Pitt Press Euclid, and to the Syndicate of the Pitt Press for their kind permission to use this proof, which is substantially the same as that given in the Pitt Press Euclid.

On BC let a rectilineal figure X be described similar to Z so that the side BC of X corresponds to the side AB of Z; and on AC let a rectilineal figure Y be described similar to Z so that the side AC of Y corresponds to the side AB of Z.

It is required to prove that

$$Z = X + Y.$$

Since Z and X are similar figures, and AB, BC are corresponding sides, therefore by Proposition 46

$\qquad Z : X = $ square on $AB : $ square on BC.

In like manner

$\qquad Z : Y = $ square on $AB : $ square on AC.

Now Z, X, Y and the squares on AB, BC, CA are all magnitudes of the same kind, viz. areas.

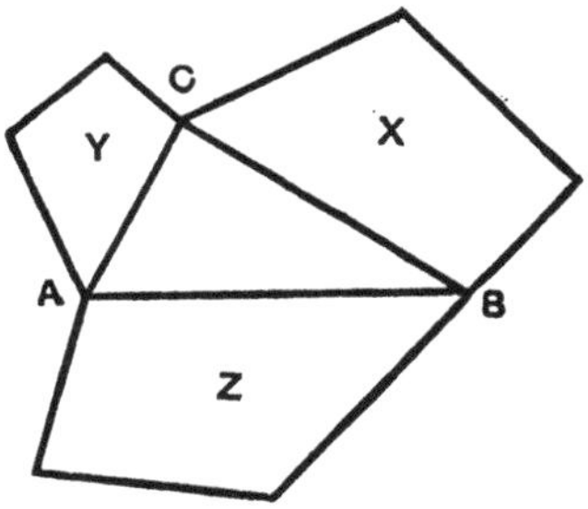

$\therefore$ by Prop. 24

$\qquad Z : $ square on $AB = \qquad X : $ square on BC,

and $\quad Z : $ square on $AB = \qquad Y : $ square on AC,

$\therefore \quad X : $ square on $BC = \qquad Y : $ square on AC.

$\therefore \quad X : $ square on $BC = X + Y : $ square on $BC + $ square on AC \qquad [Prop. 45.

$\qquad\qquad = X + Y : $ square on AB.

$\therefore \quad Z : $ square on $AB = X + Y : $ square on AB.

$\qquad\qquad \therefore \ Z = X + Y.$ \qquad\qquad\qquad\qquad [Art. 43.

Fig. 57.

Art. 137.　EXAMPLE 68.

In an acute-angled triangle similar figures are similarly described on the sides, shew that the sum of the areas of any two of them is greater than the area of the third.

Art. 138.　PROPOSITION XLIX. (Euc. VI. 25.)

ENUNCIATION. *To describe a rectilineal figure similar to one given rectilineal figure and equal in area to another given rectilineal figure.*

(In ordinary language to describe a figure having the shape of one given figure and the size of another.)

Let it be required to describe a figure similar to the figure $ABCDE$ and equal to the figure $FGHK$.

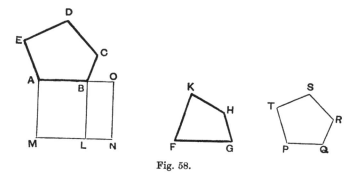

Fig. 58.

On AB describe a rectangle $ABLM$ equal to $ABCDE$.

On BL describe a rectangle $BLNO$ equal to $FGHK$.

Take PQ a mean proportional between AB and BO.   [Prop. 35.

On PQ describe a figure $PQRST$ similar to $ABCDE$, so that PQ may correspond to AB.   [Prop. 32.

It will be shewn that $PQRST$ is the figure required.

Since $AB : PQ = PQ : BO,$

          $\therefore$ square on AB : square on $PQ = AB : BO.$ [Prop. 42.

Now $AB : BO = ABLM \; : BLNO$ [Prop. 16.

                            $= ABCDE : FGHK.$

Also $ABCDE : PQRST =$ square on AB : square on $PQ.$ [Prop. 46.

          $\therefore \; ABCDE : FGHK = ABCDE : PQRST.$

                $\therefore \; FGHK = PQRST.$ [Prop. 23.

Hence $PQRST$ is equal to $FGHK$ and similar to $ABCDE$.

It is therefore the figure required.

Art. 139. *Def.* 18. FIGURES WITH SIDES RECIPROCALLY PROPORTIONAL.

A figure is said to have the two sides about one angle reciprocally proportional to the two sides about an angle of another figure when these four sides are proportional in the following manner:

          a side of the first figure : a side of the second figure

= the other side of the second figure : the other side of the first figure.

Art. 140. PROPOSITION L. (i). (Euc. VI. 14, 1st Part.)

ENUNCIATION. *Parallelograms having equal areas and having one angle of the one equal to one angle of the other have the sides about the equal angles reciprocally proportional.*

The ratio of the areas of two equiangular parallelograms is equal to the ratio of the areas of the rectangles contained by their sides.   [Prop. 41.

In this proposition it is given that the areas of the parallelograms are equal.

Hence the rectangles contained by their sides are equal.

Hence by Prop. 38 (ii)

a side of the first rectangle : a side of the second rectangle

= the other side of the second rectangle : the other side of the first rectangle.

∴ a side of the first parallelogram : a side of the second parallelogram

= the other side of the second parallelogram : the other side of the first parallelogram.

Hence the sides about the equal angles are reciprocally proportional.

Art. 141. PROPOSITION L. (ii). (Euc. VI. 14, 2nd Part.)

ENUNCIATION. *Parallelograms having one angle of the one equal to one angle of the other, and the sides about the equal angles reciprocally proportional are equal in area.*

Since the sides about the equal angles are reciprocally proportional, therefore by Prop. 38 (i) the rectangle contained by the sides of one parallelogram is equal to the rectangle contained by the sides of the other.

Therefore by Prop. 41 the parallelograms have equal areas.

Art. 142. COROLLARY TO PROP. 50. (Euc. VI. 15.)

ENUNCIATION (i). *Two triangles having equal areas and having one angle of the one equal to one angle of the other have their sides about the equal angles reciprocally proportional.*

(ii) *Two triangles which have one angle in the one equal to one angle in the other and the sides about the equal angles reciprocally proportional are equal in area.*

These propositions may be deduced from Proposition 50 by constructing the parallelograms of which the triangles are the halves.

Art. 143. EXAMPLES.

69. Triangles which have one angle in the one supplementary to one angle in the other and their sides about the supplementary angles reciprocally proportional are equal in area.

70. Triangles having equal areas and having one angle of the one supplementary to one angle of the other, have their sides about the supplementary angles reciprocally proportional.

71. If P be any point on the side AC of the triangle ABC, and if PQ be drawn parallel to BC to cut AB at Q, then if a straight line through P cut BA produced through A at R and BC at S so as to make the triangles ABC, BRS equal, prove that QR will be a third proportional to QA and QB.

72. The triangles ABC, DEF are similar, and on DE the side corresponding to AB a point K is taken so that DK is a third proportional to DE and AB, prove that the triangles ABC, DKF are equal in area.

(This is the proposition on which Euclid's proof that the areas of similar triangles are to one another as the squares described on corresponding sides is based.)

73. If a straight line DE be drawn parallel to the base BC of the triangle ABC cutting AB at D and AC at E, and if AF be drawn perpendicular to DE, prove that the rectangle $AF \cdot BC$ is double of the triangle AEB.

SECTION IX.

MISCELLANEOUS GEOMETRICAL PROPOSITIONS.

PROPOSITIONS 51—56.

Art. 144. PROPOSITION LI. (Euc. VI. B.)

ENUNCIATION. *If the vertical angle of a triangle be bisected by a straight line which also cuts the base, the rectangle contained by the sides of the triangle is equal to the rectangle contained by the segments of the base together with the square on the straight line which bisects the angle.*

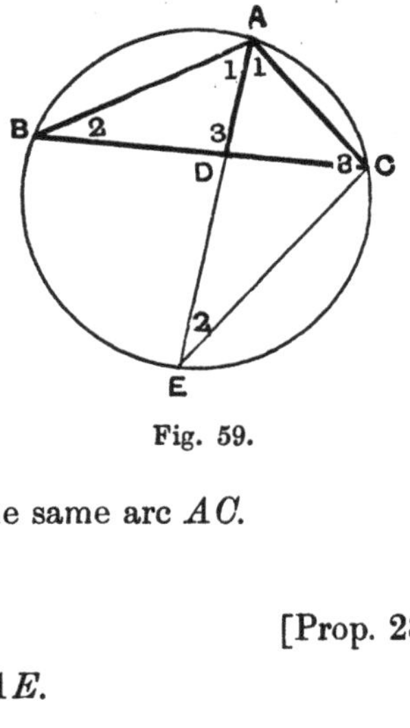

Let ABC be the triangle.

Bisect $B\hat{A}C$ by AD cutting the base BC at D.

It is required to prove that

rect. $AB.AC$ = rect. $BD.DC$ + square on AD.

Describe a circle round the triangle ABC, and let AD cut the circle at E.

Join CE.

In the triangles ABD, AEC

$$B\hat{A}D = E\hat{A}C$$

$A\hat{B}D = A\hat{E}C$, since they stand on the same arc AC.

$$\therefore A\hat{D}B = A\hat{C}E.$$

Hence the triangles are similar.   [Prop. 28.

$$\therefore BD:EC = DA:CA = AB:AE.$$

From the second and third ratios

rect. $AB.AC$ = rect. $AD.AE$ [Prop. 38 (i).

= square on AD + rect. $AD.DE$

= square on AD + rect. $BD.DC$.

Fig. 59.

Art. 145. PROPOSITION LII. (Euc. VI. C.)

ENUNCIATION. *If from any vertex of a triangle a perpendicular be drawn to the opposite side, the diameter of the circle circumscribing the triangle is a fourth proportional to the perpendicular and the sides of the triangle which meet at that vertex.*

Let ABC be a triangle.

Let BD be perpendicular to AC.

Let a circle be circumscribed about ABC.

Let BE be the diameter through B.

Join CE.

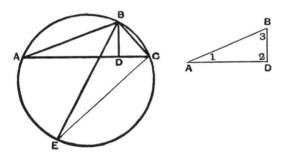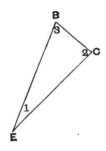

Fig. 60.

In the triangles ABD, EBC

$$B\hat{E}C = B\hat{A}D, \text{ for they stand on the same arc } BC.$$

$$B\hat{C}E = B\hat{D}A, \text{ for each is a right angle.}$$

$$\therefore \ C\hat{B}E = A\hat{B}D.$$

Hence by Prop. 28 the triangles are similar.

$$\therefore \ DB : CB = BA : BE = AD : EC.$$

From the equality of the first and second ratios it follows that the diameter BE is a fourth proportional to the perpendicular BD and the sides BC, BA.

Art. 146. EXAMPLE 74.

If D is any point on the side BC of a triangle ABC, then the diameters of the circles circumscribing the triangles ABD and ACD are proportional to the sides AB, AC.

Art. 147. PROPOSITION LIII. (Euc. VI. 30.)

ENUNCIATION. *To divide internally or externally a finite straight line in extreme and mean ratio;* i.e. so that the whole line is to one segment as that segment is to the other segment.

Let AB be the straight line, it is required to find a point C on it so that
$$AB : AC = AC : CB.$$
On AB describe the square $ABDE$.

Bisect AE at F.

Join FB.

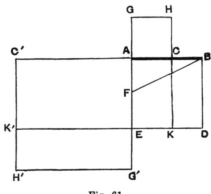

Fig. 61.

On EFA measure $FG = FG' = FB$.

On AG describe the square $ACHG$.

On AG' describe the square $AC'H'G'$.

The points C, C' fall on AB, and are the required points.

It is proved in Prop. 11 of the Second Book of Euclid that
$$\text{the square on } AC = \text{rect. } AB \cdot BC.$$
$$\therefore\ AB : AC = AC : BC. \qquad\qquad \text{[Cor. to Prop. 38.}$$

To prove the same property for the point C'.

Since AE is bisected at F and produced to G',

$\therefore$ square on $FG' =$ square on $FA +$ rect. $EG' \cdot AG'$.

$\therefore$ square on $FB\ =$ square on $FA +$ rect. $EG'H'K'$.

$\therefore$ square on FA + square on AB = square on FA + rect. $EG'H'K'$.

$\therefore$ square on AB = rect. $EG'H'K'$.

$\therefore AEDB = EG'H'K'$.

$\therefore AEDB + AEK'C' = EG'H'K' + AEK'C'$.

$\therefore BDK'C'\qquad = AC'H'G'$.

$\therefore$ rect. $BA \cdot BC'$ = square on AC'.

$\therefore AB : AC' = AC' : C'B$.   [Cor. to Prop. 38.

Art. 148.   EXAMPLE 75.

If ABC be a triangle right-angled at A, and AD be drawn perpendicular to the hypotenuse cutting it at D, and if D divide BC in extreme and mean ratio, then prove that the sides of the triangle ABC are in proportion.

Art. 149.   PROPOSITION LIV.   (Euc. VI. 24.)

ENUNCIATION. *Parallelograms about the diagonal of any parallelogram are similar to the whole and to one another.*

Let $ABCD$ be a parallelogram.

Let $AEFH$, $FKCG$ be parallelograms about the diagonal AC of the parallelogram $ABCD$.

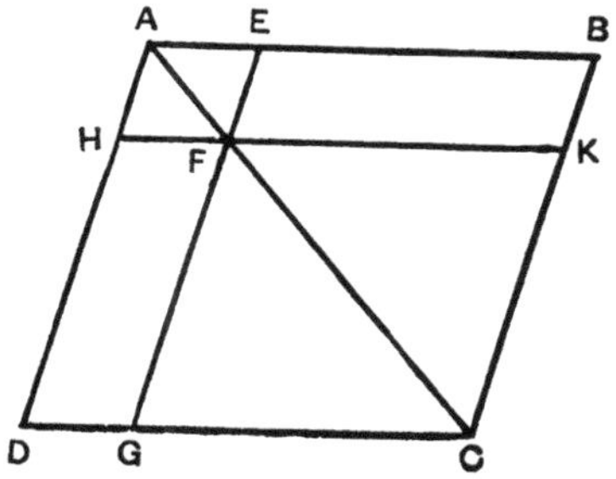

It is required to prove that they are similar to $ABCD$ and to one another.

Since EF is parallel to BC, the triangles AEF, ABC are similar.

[Cor. to Prop. 28.

$\therefore AE : AB = EF : BC = FA : CA$.

Since FH is parallel to CD, the triangles AFH, ACD are similar.

[Cor. to Prop. 28.

Fig. 62.

$\therefore FA : CA = AH : AD = HF : DC$.

Hence $AE : AB = EF : BC = FH : CD = HA : DA$.

Further $H\hat{A}E = D\hat{A}B,$

$A\hat{E}F = A\hat{B}C,$

$E\hat{F}H = B\hat{C}D,$

$F\hat{H}A = C\hat{D}A.$

H. E.   14

Hence the two sets of conditions for the similarity of $AEFH$, $ABCD$ are satisfied (Art. 77).

In like manner $FKCG$ is similar to $ABCD$.

$$\therefore \ AEFH, FKCG \text{ are similar.} \qquad \text{[Prop. 27.}$$

Art. 150. PROPOSITION LV. (Euc. VI. 26.)

ENUNCIATION. *If two similar parallelograms have a common angle and be similarly situated they are about the same diagonal.*

Let $ABCD$, $AEFH$ be two similar parallelograms having the same angle A. Let them be similarly situated, and let AB, AE be corresponding sides.

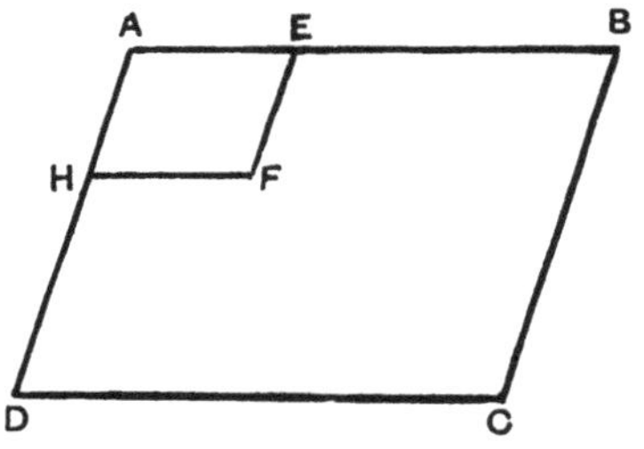

It is required to prove that the diagonals AC, AF coincide in direction.

Since the parallelograms are similar

$$A\hat{B}C = A\hat{E}F,$$
$$AB : AE = BC : EF.$$
$$\therefore \ AB : BC = AE : EF. \qquad \text{[Prop. 24.}$$

Hence the triangles ABC, AEF are similar.   [Prop. 30.

In these triangles BC, EF are corresponding sides.

Hence the angles opposite them are equal.

$$\therefore \ B\hat{A}C = E\hat{A}F.$$

Hence AC coincides in direction with AF.

Hence the parallelograms $ABCD$, $AEFH$ are about the same diagonal.

Fig. 63.

Art. 151. EXAMPLE 76.

Let the straight line AB be produced through A to P and through B to Q, so that AP is equal to BQ. On BQ, BP let similar parallelograms be similarly described, viz. $BQRS$ and $BPTU$. Prove that the parallelogram whose adjacent sides are QA, QR is equal in area to that whose adjacent sides are PA, PT.

Art. 152. PROPOSITION LVI. (Euc. VI. 27, 28, 29.)

ENUNCIATION. *If OAB be a given triangle it is required to find a point P on AB or AB produced so that if PQ be drawn parallel to OB to cut OA in Q, and if PR be drawn parallel to OA to cut OB in R, then the parallelogram PQOR may have a given area.*

There are two kinds of cases.

Case I. Suppose the point P to have been found and to lie between A and F, the middle point of AB.

Let E be the middle point of OA.

Complete the parallelogram $EAVF$.

Let QP cut FV in T.

Let PR cut EF in S and AV in U.

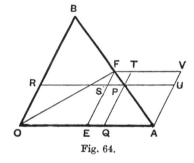

Fig. 64.

Then
$$OQPR = OESR + EQPS$$
$$= EAUS + PUVT$$
$$= EAVF - SPTF$$
$$= \triangle OAF - SPTF.$$

Hence if P be between A and F the area $OQPR$ is less than the triangle OAF. (This is equivalent to the result of Euc. VI. 27.)

Hence
$$SPTF = \triangle OAF - OQPR$$
$$= \tfrac{1}{2} (\text{given triangle } OAB) - (\text{a given area}).$$

Hence the parallelogram $SPTF$ has a known area.

It is also known to be similar to the known parallelogram $EAVF$.

Hence it can be constructed by Prop. 49, and if it be placed so that the side corresponding to FV falls along FV, and the side corresponding to FE falls along FE, then its diagonal will fall on FA by Prop. 55.

Hence the position of P is known.

(This is equivalent to the result of Euc. VI. 28.)

In order that the construction for P may be possible it is necessary that the given area should not exceed half the given triangle OAB.

The above construction applies only to the case where P lies between A and F, the middle point of AB.

If P be one position of the required point, let a point P' be taken on FB so that $PF = P'F$, and let Q', R', S', T' be the points corresponding to Q, R, S, T.

Then the parallelograms $SPTF$, $S'P'T'F$ are equal.

Hence the parallelograms $OQPR$, $OQ'P'R'$ are equal.

Hence P' is another position of the required point.

Case II. Let P be on BA produced through A, and let the same construction be made.

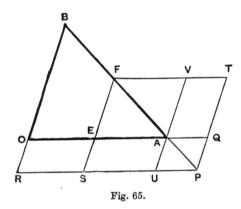

Fig. 65.

Then
$$OQPR = OESR + EQPS$$
$$= EAUS + PUVT$$
$$= SPTF - EAVF$$
$$= SPTF - \triangle OAF.$$
$$\therefore SPTF = \triangle OAF + OQPR$$
$$= \tfrac{1}{2} \text{ (given triangle } OAB) + \text{(a given area)}.$$

Hence the parallelogram $SPTF$ has a known area.

It is also known to be similar to the known parallelogram $EAVF$.

Hence it can be constructed by Prop. 49, and if it be placed so that the side corresponding to FV falls along FV, and the side corresponding to FE falls along FE, then its diagonal will fall along FA by Prop. 55.

Hence the position of P is known.

(This is equivalent to the result of Euc. VI. 29.)

In this case the construction is always possible for all magnitudes of the given area.

If P be one position of the required point, and a point P' be taken on FB produced through B so that $P'F = PF$, then it may be shown that P' is another position of the required point.

It results from Cases I and II that if the given area be less than half the given triangle OAB there are *four* solutions of the problem, viz. P may be between A and F or between F and B, or on BA produced through A, or on AB produced through B.

If the given area be equal to half the triangle OAB there are *three* solutions, viz. P may be at F, or on BA produced through A, or on AB produced through B.

If the given area be greater than half the triangle OAB there are *two* solutions, viz. P may be on BA produced through A, or on AB produced through B.

SECTION X.

THE REMAINING IMPORTANT PROPOSITIONS IN THE THEORY OF
RATIO, WITH GEOMETRICAL APPLICATIONS.

PROPOSITIONS 57—64.

Art. 153. PROPOSITION LVII. (Euc. V. 23.)

ENUNCIATION. *If A, B, C are three magnitudes of the same kind,*

if   *T, U, V are three magnitudes of the same kind,*

if $A : B = U : V,$

and $B : C = T : U,$

prove that $A : C = T : V.$

Compare $A : C$ with any rational fraction $\dfrac{s}{r}$.

It is necessary to consider only the two cases   [Art. 48.

$$(1) \quad A : C > \frac{s}{r}.$$

$$(2) \quad A : C < \frac{s}{r}.$$

In case (1) $A : C > \dfrac{s}{r},$

$$\therefore \ rA > sC.$$

$\therefore \ rA - sC$ is a magnitude of the same kind as B.

Hence by Archimedes' Axiom an integer n exists, such that

$$n(rA - sC) > B,$$
$$\therefore nrA > nsC + B.$$

Hence an integer t exists, such that

$$nrA > tB > nsC. \qquad \text{[Prop. 8.}$$
$$\therefore nrA > tB,$$
$$\therefore A : B > \frac{t}{nr};$$

but
$$A : B = U : V,$$
$$\therefore U : V > \frac{t}{nr},$$
$$\therefore nrU > tV. \qquad \text{(I)*}$$

Since
$$tB > nsC,$$
$$\therefore B : C > \frac{ns}{t};$$

but
$$B : C = T : U,$$
$$\therefore T : U > \frac{ns}{t},$$
$$\therefore tT > nsU; \qquad \text{(II)*}$$
$$\therefore rtT > rnsU,$$

and from (I)
$$snrU > stV,$$
$$\therefore rtT > stV,$$
$$\therefore rT > sV,$$
$$\therefore T : V > \frac{s}{r}.$$

Hence if
$$A : C > \frac{s}{r}, \text{ then } T : V > \frac{s}{r}.$$

In case (2)
$$A : C < \frac{s}{r},$$
$$\therefore rA < sC.$$

$\therefore sC - rA$ is a magnitude of the same kind as B.

___

* In the above proposition the inequalities (I) and (II) are transformed so that the multiples of U, which occurs in both, are the same. The inequalities (III) and (IV) below are treated in the same way.

Hence by Archimedes' Axiom an integer n exists, such that

$$n\,(sC - rA) > B,$$

$$\therefore\ nsC > nrA + B.$$

Hence a multiple of B exists, say tB, such that

$$nrA < tB < nsC.$$
[Prop. 8.

Since $\qquad\qquad nrA < tB,$

$$\therefore\ A : B < \frac{t}{nr};$$

but $\qquad\qquad A : B = U : V,$

$$\therefore\ U : V < \frac{t}{nr},$$

$$\therefore\ nrU < tV.$$
(III)

Since $\qquad\qquad tB < nsC,$

$$\therefore\ B : C < \frac{ns}{t}.$$

But $\qquad\qquad B : C = T : U,$

$$\therefore\ T : U < \frac{ns}{t},$$

$$\therefore\ tT < nsU.$$
(IV)

From (III) $\qquad\qquad snrU < stV.$

From (IV) $\qquad\qquad rtT < rnsU,$

$$\therefore\ rtT < stV,$$

$$\therefore\ rT < sV,$$

$$\therefore\ T : V < \frac{s}{r}.$$

Hence if $\qquad A : C < \frac{s}{r},\ \text{then}\ T : V < \frac{s}{r}.$

But if $\qquad A : C > \frac{s}{r},\ \text{then}\ T : V > \frac{s}{r}.$

Consequently $\qquad A : C = T : V.$
[Art. 48.

Art. 154. PROPOSITION LVIII. (Euc. V. 18.)

ENUNCIATION. *If two ratios are equal, the ratio of the sum of the antecedent and consequent of the first ratio to the consequent of the first ratio is equal to the ratio of the sum of the antecedent and consequent of the second ratio to the consequent of the second ratio;*

i.e. if $A : B = X : Y,$

to prove that $A + B : B = X + Y : Y.$

Compare the ratio $A + B : B$ with the rational fraction $\dfrac{s}{r}$.

There are three alternatives

$$(1)\quad A + B : B > \frac{s}{r},$$

$$(2)\quad A + B : B = \frac{s}{r},$$

$$(3)\quad A + B : B < \frac{s}{r}.$$

In case (1) $A + B : B > \dfrac{s}{r},$

$$\therefore\ r\,(A + B) > sB.$$

In this case it is necessary to consider separately the cases

$$r < s, \quad r = s, \quad r > s.$$

If $r < s$, the last inequality can be written

$$rA > (s - r)\,B.$$

$$\therefore\ A : B > \frac{s - r}{r};$$

but $A : B = X : Y,$

$$\therefore\ X : Y > \frac{s - r}{r},$$

$$\therefore\ rX > (s - r)\,Y,$$

$$\therefore\ r\,(X + Y) > sY,$$

$$\therefore\ X + Y : Y > \frac{s}{r}.$$

H. E.   15

If $r = s$, then $$rY = sY$$

and $$\therefore r(X + Y) > sY,$$

$$\therefore X + Y : Y > \frac{s}{r}.$$

If $r > s$, then $$rY > sY,$$

$$\therefore r(X + Y) > sY,$$

$$\therefore X + Y : Y > \frac{s}{r}.$$

In case (2) $$A + B : B = \frac{s}{r},$$

$$\therefore r(A + B) = sB.$$

This is impossible unless $r < s$.

Hence it can be written

$$rA = (s - r)B,$$

$$\therefore A : B = \frac{s - r}{r};$$

but $$A : B = X : Y,$$

$$\therefore X : Y = \frac{s - r}{r},$$

$$\therefore rX = (s - r)Y,$$

$$\therefore r(X + Y) = sY,$$

$$\therefore X + Y : Y = \frac{s}{r}.$$

In case (3) $$A + B : B < \frac{s}{r},$$

$$\therefore r(A + B) < sB.$$

This is impossible unless $r < s$.

$$\therefore rA < (s - r)B,$$

$$\therefore A : B < \frac{s - r}{r}.$$

But $$A : B = X : Y,$$

$$\therefore X : Y < \frac{s - r}{r},$$

$$\therefore rX < (s - r)Y,$$

$$\therefore \; r(X+Y) < sY,$$

$$\therefore \; X+Y:Y < \frac{s}{r}.$$

Hence, if $\quad A+B:B > \dfrac{s}{r}$, then $X+Y:Y > \dfrac{s}{r}$,

if $\qquad\quad A+B:B = \dfrac{s}{r}$, then $X+Y:Y = \dfrac{s}{r}$,

if $\qquad\quad A+B:B < \dfrac{s}{r}$, then $X+Y:Y < \dfrac{s}{r}$.

$$\therefore \; A+B:B = X+Y:Y.$$

Art. 155. EXAMPLES.

77. If ABC be a triangle right-angled at C, and if AD bisect the angle BAC cutting BC at D, prove that

$$AC:CD = AC+AB:BC.$$

(By means of this proposition Archimedes showed that the length of the circumference of a circle was less than $3\frac{1}{7}$ times its diameter.)

78. If ABC be a triangle right-angled at C, if AD bisect the angle BAC and cut BC at D, and if BE be drawn perpendicular to AD cutting it at E, prove that

$$AE:EB = AC+AB:BC.$$

(By means of this proposition Archimedes showed that the length of the circumference of a circle was greater than $3\frac{10}{71}$ times its diameter.)

Art. 156. PROPOSITION LIX. (Euc. V. I7.)

ENUNCIATION. *If two ratios are equal, then the ratio of the difference of the antecedent and consequent of the first ratio to the consequent of the first ratio is equal to the ratio of the difference of the antecedent and consequent of the second ratio to the consequent of the second ratio;*

i.e. if $\qquad\qquad A:B = X:Y,$

then $\qquad\qquad A \sim B:B = X \sim Y:Y.$

It is necessary to consider separately the cases

$$A > B,$$
$$A = B,$$
$$A < B.$$

If $A > B$, and therefore $X > Y$, then it is required to prove that
$$A - B : B = X - Y : Y.$$

Compare $A - B : B$ with the rational fraction $\frac{s}{r}$.

There are three cases

$$(1) \quad A - B : B > \frac{s}{r}.$$

$$(2) \quad A - B : B = \frac{s}{r}.$$

$$(3) \quad A - B : B < \frac{s}{r}.$$

In case (1)
$$A - B : B > \frac{s}{r},$$
$$\therefore r(A - B) > sB,$$
$$\therefore rA > (r + s)B,$$
$$\therefore A : B > \frac{r + s}{r};$$

but
$$A : B = X : Y,$$
$$\therefore X : Y > \frac{r + s}{r},$$
$$\therefore rX > (r + s)Y,$$
$$\therefore r(X - Y) > sY,$$
$$\therefore X - Y : Y > \frac{s}{r}.$$

In case (2)
$$A - B : B = \frac{s}{r},$$
$$\therefore r(A - B) = sB,$$
$$\therefore rA = (r + s)B,$$
$$\therefore A : B = \frac{r + s}{r};$$

but
$$A : B = X : Y,$$
$$\therefore X : Y = \frac{r + s}{r},$$
$$\therefore rX = (r + s)Y,$$

$$\therefore \ r(X - Y) = sY,$$

$$\therefore \ X - Y : Y = \frac{s}{r}.$$

In case (3)

$$A - B : B < \frac{s}{r},$$

$$\therefore \ r(A - B) < sB,$$

$$\therefore \ rA < (r + s) B,$$

$$\therefore \ A : B < \frac{r + s}{r}.$$

But

$$A : B = X : Y,$$

$$\therefore \ X : Y < \frac{r + s}{r},$$

$$\therefore \ rX < (r + s) Y,$$

$$\therefore \ r(X - Y) < sY,$$

$$\therefore \ X - Y : Y < \frac{s}{r}.$$

Hence if

$$A - B : B > \frac{s}{r}, \ \text{then} \ X - Y : Y > \frac{s}{r},$$

if

$$A - B : B = \frac{s}{r}, \ \text{then} \ X - Y : Y = \frac{s}{r},$$

if

$$A - B : B < \frac{s}{r}, \ \text{then} \ X - Y : Y < \frac{s}{r}.$$

$$\therefore \ A - B : B = X - Y : Y.$$

If $A = B$, then $X = Y$.

Hence the difference of A and B, and the difference of X and Y, are both zero.

Hence the first term of each of the ratios $A - B : B$ and $X - Y : Y$ is zero, and the ratios may be considered to be the same.

If $A < B$, and therefore $X < Y$, then it is required to show that

$$B - A : B = Y - X : Y.$$

This may be proved independently as in the first case, or may be deduced from it.

For if

$$A : B = X : Y,$$

then

$$B : A = Y : X. \qquad\qquad \text{[Prop. 21.}$$

$$\therefore \ B - A : A = Y - X : X, \ \text{by Case 1.}$$

But

$$A : B = X : Y.$$

$$\therefore \ B - A : B = Y - X : Y. \qquad\qquad \text{[Prop. 37.}$$

Art. 157. EXAMPLES.

79. Prove the last case of Proposition 59 directly in a manner similar to that adopted for the first case.

80. If $A : B = X : Y$, and $A > B$, prove that
$$A : A - B = X : X - Y.$$

81. If $A : B = B : C$, and $A > B$, prove that
$$A - C : A - B = B + C : B.$$

Art. 158. PROPOSITION LX.

ENUNCIATION. *If* $\qquad A : B = X : Y,$

prove that $\qquad A \sim B : A + B = X \sim Y : X + Y.$

If $\qquad A : B = X : Y,$

then $\qquad A + B : B = X + Y : Y.$ [Prop. 58.

$\qquad \therefore B : A + B = Y : X + Y.$ [Prop. 21.

Also $\qquad A \sim B : B = X \sim Y : Y.$ [Prop. 59.

$\qquad \therefore A \sim B : A + B = X \sim Y : X + Y.$ [Prop. 37.

Art. 159. PROPOSITION LXI.

ENUNCIATION. *If A, B, C, D be four harmonic points, A and C being conjugate, and if O be the middle point of AC, then OC is a mean proportional between OB and OD.*

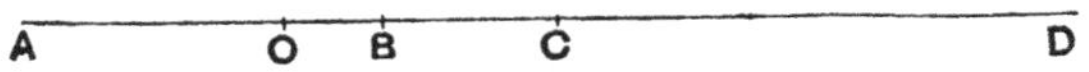

Fig. 66.

Since A divides BD in the same ratio as C does,
$$AB : AD = BC : CD.$$
$$\therefore AB : BC = AD : CD.$$ [Prop. 24.
$$\therefore AB - BC : AB + BC = AD - CD : AD + CD.$$ [Prop. 60.
$$\therefore 2OB : 2OC = 2OC : 2OD.$$
$$\therefore OB : OC = OC : OD.$$ [Prop. 15.

$\therefore OC$ is a mean proportional between OB and OD.

Art. 160. EXAMPLES.

82. Prove that if a circle be drawn through two points which are inverse with regard to a second circle, then the two circles cut each other at right angles.

83. If A, B, C, D be four harmonic points, and if O be the middle point of AC, show that a circle can be drawn with centre O so as to cut at right angles any circle that can be drawn through B and D in the plane of the circle whose centre is O.

84. If the diagonals AC, BD of the quadrilateral $ABCD$ intersect at E and a straight line EG be drawn parallel to one of the sides AB meeting the opposite side CD in G and the third diagonal (i.e. the straight line joining H the intersection of AB and CD to I the intersection of AD and BC) in J, then EJ is bisected at G.

[If EG cut AD in K and BC in L, prove that

$$AB : BH = KL : LJ = EL : LG = KE : EG.]$$

Hence by the aid of Ex. 50 show that HA, HE, HC, HI are four harmonic lines.

Art. 161. PROPOSITION LXII. (Euc. V. 24.)

ENUNCIATION. *If* $A : C = X : Z,$

and $B : C = Y : Z,$

prove that $A + B : C = X + Y : Z.$

Since $B : C = Y : Z,$

$\therefore C : B = Z : Y,$ [Prop. 21.

but $A : C = X : Z,$

$\therefore A : B = X : Y,$ [Prop. 37.

$\therefore A + B : B = X + Y : Y,$ [Prop. 58.

but $B : C = Y : Z,$

$\therefore A + B : C = X + Y : Z.$ [Prop. 37.

Art. 162. PROPOSITION LXIII. (Euc. V. 4.)

ENUNCIATION. *If* $A : B = X : Y,$

to prove that $rA : sB = rX : sY.$

Compare the ratio $rA : sB$ with any rational fraction $\dfrac{p}{q}$.

There are three cases

$$(1) \quad rA : sB > \frac{p}{q},$$

$$(2) \quad rA : sB = \frac{p}{q},$$

$$(3) \quad rA : sB < \frac{p}{q}.$$

In case (1)

$$rA : sB > \frac{p}{q},$$

$$\therefore q(rA) > p(sB),$$

$$\therefore qrA > psB,$$

$$\therefore A : B > \frac{ps}{qr}.$$

But

$$A : B = X : Y,$$

$$\therefore X : Y > \frac{ps}{qr},$$

$$\therefore qrX > psY,$$

$$\therefore q(rX) > p(sY),$$

$$\therefore rX : sY > \frac{p}{q}.$$

Hence if $\quad rA : sB > \dfrac{p}{q},$ then $rX : sY > \dfrac{p}{q}.$

In like manner it can be shown that

if $\qquad rA : sB = \dfrac{p}{q},$ then $rX : sY = \dfrac{p}{q},$

and if $\qquad rA : sB < \dfrac{p}{q},$ then $rX : sY < \dfrac{p}{q}.$

$$\therefore rA : sB = rX : sY.$$

Art. 163.   EXAMPLE 85.

Prove the converse of Proposition 63, viz.

If $\qquad rA : sB = rX : sY,$

then $\qquad A : B = X : Y.$

Art. 164.   PROPOSITION LXIV.

ENUNCIATION. *If K, L, M, P be four straight lines in proportion, if the lengths of L and M be fixed, if the length of K can be made smaller than that of any line however small, to show that the length of P can be made greater than that of any line Q, however great Q may be.*

By Archimedes' Axiom (Art. 22), it is always possible to find an integer r such that

$$rM > Q.$$

Now divide L into r equal parts, and take K smaller than one of these equal parts.

Then $rK < L.$

Now $K : L = M : P.$

$$\therefore \ rK : L = rM : P. \qquad\qquad \text{[Prop. 63.}$$

Now $rK < L.$

$$\therefore \ rM < P.$$

But $Q < rM.$

$$\therefore \ Q < P.$$

Art. 165.   EXAMPLE 86.

If K, L, M, P be four straight lines in proportion, if the lengths of L, M be fixed, and if the length of K can be made greater than that of any line however great, show that the length of P can be made smaller than that of any line Q however small.

SECTION XI.

Art. 166. PROPOSITION LXV. (Euc. V. 19.)

ENUNCIATION. *If A, B, C, D are magnitudes of the same kind, and*

$$A : B = C : D,$$

prove that
$$A \sim C : B \sim D = A : B.$$

$$A : B = C : D,$$

$$\therefore \ A : C = B : D, \qquad\qquad\qquad \text{[Prop. 24.}$$

$$\therefore \ A \sim C : C = B \sim D : D, \qquad\qquad \text{[Prop. 59.}$$

$$\therefore \ A \sim C : B \sim D = C : D, \qquad\qquad \text{[Prop. 24.}$$

$$\therefore \ A \sim C : B \sim D = A : B.$$

Art. 167. EXAMPLE 87.

If X, A, S, A' are four harmonic points, A and A' being conjugate, and if C be the middle point of AA', prove that

$$SA : AX = CS : CA = CA : CX.$$

Art. 168. PROPOSITION LXVI. (Euc. V. 25.)

ENUNCIATION. *If four magnitudes of the same kind are proportional, then the greatest and least of them together are greater than the sum of the other two.*

Let
$$A : B = C : D.$$

Suppose A the greatest of the four magnitudes.

Then $$A > B.$$

$$\therefore A : B > \frac{1}{1}.$$

$$\therefore C : D > \frac{1}{1}.$$

$$\therefore C > D.$$

Again $$\because A : B = C : D.$$

Now $$A > C.$$

$$\therefore B > D. \qquad \text{[Art. 70.}$$

Hence D is the least of the four magnitudes.

Hence it is required to prove that

$$A + D > B + C.$$

Since $$A : B = C : D,$$

$$\therefore A - B : B = C - D : D. \qquad \text{[Prop. 59.}$$

$$\therefore A - B : C - D = B : D. \qquad \text{[Prop. 24.}$$

Now $$B > D.$$

$$\therefore A - B > C - D.$$

$$\therefore A + D > B + C.$$

Art. 169. EXAMPLE 88.

If three quantities be in proportion, show that the sum of the extremes will exceed double the mean.

NOTES.

Props. 1—5 relate to certain simple cases of the application of the Commutative, Associative and Distributive Laws, with which the reader who has commenced elementary Algebra is already familiar.

Prop. I. $$r(A + B) = rA + rB.$$

Treating $A + B$ as the multiplicand,

and r as the multiplier,

it is seen that the *multiplicand* is divided (or distributed) into its parts A, B.

Prop. II. $$(a + b) R = aR + bR.$$

Treating $a + b$ as the multiplier,

and R as the multiplicand,

it is seen that the *multiplier* is distributed into its parts a, b.

Prop. III. If $$A > B,$$
$$r(A - B) = rA - rB.$$

Here the *multiplicand* $A - B$ is distributed into its parts A, B.

Prop. IV. If $$a > b,$$
$$(a - b) R = aR - bR.$$

Here the *multiplier* $a - b$ is distributed into its parts a, b.

Prop. V. $$r(sA) = (rs) A = (sr) A = s(rA).$$

This illustrates both the Commutative and Associative Laws.

The fact $$(rs) A = (sr) A$$

illustrates the Commutative Law.

The fact that $$r(sA) = (rs) A$$

and the fact that $$(sr) A = s(rA)$$

both illustrate the Associative Law.

If Propositions 1—4, 6, 15 and Art. 31 be arranged in parallel columns, thus:—

I. $r(A + B) = rA + rB.$ II. $(a + b) R = aR + bR.$

III. $r(A - B) = rA - rB.$ IV. $(a - b) R = aR - bR.$

VI (i).   If $A \gtreqless B,$ VI (iii).   If $a \gtreqless b,$
then $rA \gtreqless rB.$ then $aR \gtreqless bR.$

VI (ii).   If $rA \gtreqless rB,$ VI (iv).   If $aR \gtreqless bR,$
then $A \gtreqless B.$ then $a \gtreqless b.$

XV. $A : B = nA : nB.$ Art. 31 $a : b = aN : bN.$

Then the two propositions in any one line are related to each other in such a manner that magnitudes in either are replaced by whole numbers in the other.

NOTE 2. On Props. I. and II.

Art. 171. A more formal proof of Proposition I. will now be given.

The Commutative Law is

$$X + Y = Y + X. \tag{I}$$

The Associative Law is

$$(X + Y) + Z = X + (Y + Z). \tag{II}$$

The argument will be followed more easily if the associative law be also written

$$X + (Y + Z) = (X + Y) + Z. \tag{III}$$

When used in the form (II) the first term on the left $X + Y$ is broken into two parts, and the term Y is added to the second term Z on the left.

When used in the form (III) the second term on the left $Y + Z$ is broken into two parts, and the term Y is added to the first term X on the left.

Art. 172. LEMMA.

To prove $(rA + rB) + (A + B) = (r + 1) A + (r + 1) B.$

Putting $X = rA + rB, \quad Y = A, \quad Z = B$ in (III),

$$(rA + rB) + (A + B) = [(rA + rB) + A] + B.$$

Putting $X = rA, \quad Y = rB, \quad Z = A$ in (II),

$$[(rA + rB) + A] = rA + (rB + A)$$
$$= rA + (A + rB) \text{ by (I).}$$

Putting $\qquad X = rA, \quad Y = A, \quad Z = rB$ in (III),

$$rA + (A + rB) = (rA + A) + rB.$$

$$\therefore \; [(rA + rB) + A] = (rA + A) + rB.$$

$$\therefore \; (rA + rB) + (A + B) = [(rA + A) + rB] + B.$$

Putting $\qquad X = (rA + A), \quad Y = rB, \quad Z = B$ in (II),

$$[(rA + A) + rB] + B = (rA + A) + (rB + B).$$

$$\therefore \; (rA + rB) + (A + B) = (rA + A) + (rB + B).$$

But by Art. 3 $\qquad\qquad rA + A = (r + 1)A,$

and $\qquad\qquad\qquad\qquad rB + B = (r + 1)B.$

$$\therefore \; (rA + rB) + (A + B) = (r + 1)A + (r + 1)B.$$

Art. 173. To prove $\qquad r(A + B) = rA + rB.$

Now since $\qquad\qquad\qquad 2X = X + X,$

$$\therefore \; 2(A + B) = (A + B) + (A + B).$$

But by putting $r = 1$ in Art. 172

$$(A + B) + (A + B) = 2A + 2B,$$

$$\therefore \; 2(A + B) = 2A + 2B.$$

Again since $\qquad\qquad\qquad 3X = 2X + X,$

$$\therefore \; 3(A + B) = 2(A + B) + (A + B),$$

$$\therefore \; 3(A + B) = (2A + 2B) + (A + B)$$

$$= 3A + 3B \text{ by putting } r = 2 \text{ in Art. 172.}$$

Proceeding thus suppose it has been proved that for some positive integer t

$$t(A + B) = tA + tB.$$

Since $\qquad\qquad\qquad (t + 1)X = tX + X,$

$$\therefore \; (t + 1)(A + B)$$

$$= t(A + B) + (A + B)$$

$$= (tA + tB) + (A + B) \text{ by hypothesis}$$

$$= (t + 1)A + (t + 1)B,$$

as is seen by putting $r = t$ in Art. 172,

i.e. $\qquad\qquad (t + 1)(A + B) = (t + 1)A + (t + 1)B.$

Hence if $r(A + B) = rA + rB$, for any integral value of r, it is true for the next integral value.

But it is true for $r = 2$ and $r = 3$, therefore it is true for $r = 4$, therefore for $r = 5$ and so on it is true for every positive integral value.

Art. 174. A more formal proof of Prop. II. will now be given.

To prove $aR + bR = (a + b)R,$

$$aR + R = (a + 1)R \text{ by Art. 3,}$$

$$\therefore (aR + R) + R = (a + 1)R + R = (a + 2)R \text{ by Art. 3.}$$

Now $(aR + R) + R = aR + (R + R)$ by (II) of Art. 171

$$= aR + 2R,$$

$$\therefore aR + 2R = (a + 2)R,$$

$$\therefore (aR + 2R) + R = (a + 2)R + R = (a + 3)R \text{ by Art. 3.}$$

Now $(aR + 2R) + R = aR + (2R + R)$ by (II) of Art. 171

$$= aR + 3R,$$

$$\therefore aR + 3R = (a + 3)R.$$

Suppose it has been proved by successive steps that

$$aR + cR = (a + c)R.$$

Then $(aR + cR) + R = (a + c)R + R = (a + c + 1)R.$ [Art. 3.

But $(aR + cR) + R = aR + (cR + R)$ by (II) of Art. 171

$$= aR + (c + 1)R,$$

$$\therefore aR + (c + 1)R = (a + c + 1)R.$$

Hence if $aR + cR = (a + c)R,$

then $aR + (c + 1)R = (a + c + 1)R.$

Now it has been proved that

$$aR + 3R = (a + 3)R,$$

$$\therefore aR + 4R = (a + 4)R,$$

and so on it follows that

$$aR + bR = (a + b)R,$$

where a, b are any positive integers.

Art. 175. NOTE 3. ON ART. 46.

Euclid's Eleventh Proposition of his Fifth Book is as follows :—

If the ratio of $A : B$ is the same as that of $C : D,$

and if the ratio of $A : B$ is the same as that of $E : F,$

then the ratio of $C : D$ is the same as that of $E : F.$

As remarked in the preface, if a ratio is treated as a magnitude, then this merely expresses that if $X = Y,$ and if $X = Z,$ then $Y = Z.$

Euclid in his proof takes a different point of view; which may be expressed thus :—

If the magnitudes A, B, C, D satisfy the conditions of the Fifth Definition of the Fifth Book; and if the magnitudes A, B, E, F also satisfy them, then will the magnitudes C, D, E, F satisfy them.

The proof, stated in the manner of this book, will be as follows :—

Take any rational fraction $\dfrac{s}{r}$.

Compare with it the ratio $C : D$.

Then (1) $C : D$ may be greater than $\dfrac{s}{r}$,

or (2) $C : D$ may be equal to $\dfrac{s}{r}$,

or (3) $C : D$ may be less than $\dfrac{s}{r}$.

Take the case (1) $\qquad\qquad C : D > \dfrac{s}{r}$.

Then since A, B, C, D satisfy the conditions of Euclid's Fifth Definition

$$A : B > \frac{s}{r},$$

and then since A, B, E, F satisfy the conditions of Euclid's Fifth Definition,

$$\therefore\ E : F > \frac{s}{r}.$$

Hence if $\qquad\qquad C : D > \dfrac{s}{r},\ \text{then}\ E : F > \dfrac{s}{r}.$

Similarly if $\qquad\quad C : D = \dfrac{s}{r},\ \text{then}\ E : F = \dfrac{s}{r},$

and if $\qquad\qquad\ C : D < \dfrac{s}{r},\ \text{then}\ E : F < \dfrac{s}{r}:$

$$\therefore\ C : D = E : F. \qquad\qquad \text{[Art. 46.}$$

Art. 176.   NOTE 4.   Euclid's Definition of Ratio.

Euclid's Definition of Ratio (the third Definition of the Fifth Book) is as follows :

Λόγος ἐστὶ δύο μεγεθῶν ὁμογενῶν ἡ κατὰ πηλικότητα πρὸς ἄλληλα ποιὰ σχέσις.

De Morgan translates it thus:

"Ratio is a certain mutual habitude of two magnitudes of the same kind depending on their quantuplicity."

The word "quantuplicity" which represents the Greek "$\pi\eta\lambda\iota\kappa\acute{o}\tau\eta\varsigma$" is especially difficult. It contains the idea of relative magnitude.

De Morgan defines Ratio as Relative Magnitude on page 63 of his *Treatise on the Connexion of Number and Magnitude.*

Art. 177. NOTE 5. INCOMMENSURABLE MAGNITUDES. (See Art. 43.)

To prove that incommensurable magnitudes exist, it is sufficient to show this in a particular case.

The case which will be selected is that of a side and a diagonal of a square.

Let X be the side, and Y the diagonal of the square $OABC$.

Along the diagonal BO take $BD = BA$. Draw DE perpendicular to BO to meet OA at E.

Then the right-angled triangles BEA, BED have the hypotenuse BE in common, and one side $BA =$ one side BD.

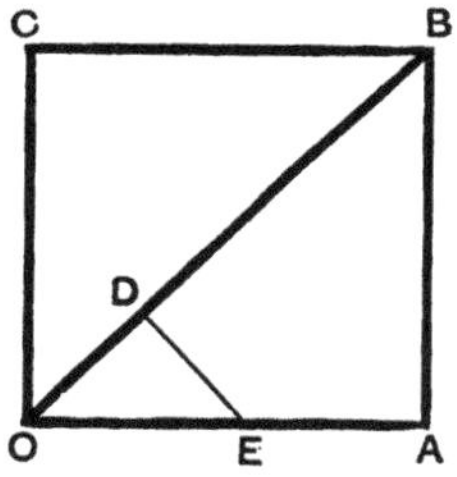

Hence they are congruent.

$$\therefore EA = ED.$$

Again DOE is an isosceles right-angled triangle,

$$\therefore ED = DO.$$

Now
$$OB = BD + DO$$
$$= 1\,(OA) + OD,$$
$$OA = OE + EA = OE + OD.$$

Fig. 67.

Now let
$$OA = X, \quad OB = Y.$$

Call
$$OD = X_1, \quad OE = Y_1.$$

Then
$$Y = 1\,(X) + X_1,$$
$$X = X_1 + Y_1.$$

Hence if $\qquad$ X and Y have a common measure,

$\qquad\qquad\qquad\quad$ X_1 is measured by it,

and $\qquad\qquad\quad$ $\therefore Y_1$ is measured by it.

Hence if X and Y have a common measure, this common measure also measures X_1 and Y_1.

Now X_1 and Y_1 are the side and diagonal of a smaller square.

But this is a process which can be continued without limit.

It will now be shown that any common measure of X and Y is also a common measure of the side and diagonal of a square, whose side can be made as small as we please.

Suppose that by repeating the construction on the square whose side is X_1, another square is obtained whose side is X_2 and diagonal Y_2 and so on.

Now
$$X = X_1 + Y_1,$$

but
$$Y_1 > X_1.$$
$$\therefore \ X > 2X_1.$$

Similarly
$$X_1 > 2X_2,$$

and so on.

Hence after repeating the process n times, it follows that
$$X > 2^n X_n.$$

But
$$2^n = (1+1)^n > 1 + n > n,$$
$$\therefore \ X > nX_n.$$

Hence the common measure of X and Y, if it exist, is not greater than X_n and $\therefore$ less than $\dfrac{X}{n}$ however large n may be.

Now if X, Y have a common measure G, it is always possible by Archimedes' Axiom to find an integer n, such that
$$nG > X,$$
$$\therefore \ G > \frac{X}{n},$$

which is contrary to what is proved above.

Hence X and Y have no common measure.

Hence the side and diagonal of a square have no common measure.

Hence incommensurable magnitudes exist.

Art. 178.   NOTE 6.   On Prop. 24.

In order to complete the proof of Prop. 24 without using Prop. 14 it is necessary to show directly that

if
$$A : B = C : D,$$

and if $rA = sC$, then $rB = sD$.

If	$rA = sC,$	
then	$rA : B = sC : B.$	
Now	$A : B = C : D,$	
	$\therefore\ rA : B = rC : D.$	[Prop. 63.
	$\therefore\ sC : B = rC : D.$	

The required result follows from this by so altering the terms of the ratios that the 1st term is the same in each.

Now	$sC : B = rsC : rB,$	[Prop. 15.
and	$rC : D = srC : sD.$	[Prop. 15.
	$\therefore\ rsC : rB = srC : sD.$	
	$\therefore\ rB = sD.$	[Prop. 23.

ANOTHER PROOF.

Since	$A : B = C : D,$	
	$\therefore\ rA : rB = A : B,$	[Prop. 15.
and	$sC : sD = C : D,$	[Prop. 15.
	$\therefore\ rA : rB = sC : sD.$	
But	$rA = sC,$	
	$\therefore\ rB = sD.$	[Prop. 23.

Art. 179. NOTE 7. ON PROP. 26.

The 26th Proposition is a very suggestive one. It not only leads naturally to the consideration of the point at infinity on a straight line, which is briefly mentioned below, but also to the consideration of negative ratios (which are not treated in this book).

It has been shown that if $K : L$ is not a ratio of equality, then there is one way of dividing AB internally and one way of dividing it externally in the ratio $K : L$.

Let the internal point of division be C, and the external point of division C', then it appears from the proof of Prop. 26 that C and C' always lie on the same side of O, the middle point of AB.

Further it follows from Prop. 61 that

$$\text{the rect. } OC \cdot OC' = \text{the square on } OA.$$

Now suppose that the length of K is fixed, and let the effect of diminishing the length of L down to equality with that of K be investigated.

Then AC and CB tend to become equal, and therefore C approaches O, and by making the difference of K and L sufficiently small the length OC may be made smaller than any length however small; and therefore by Prop. 64 the length of OC' can be made greater than any length however great.

Similar conclusions can be drawn from the case in which K is greater than L, except that C and C' are on the same side of O as B.

When however $K = L$, the internal point of division is the middle point, but the external point of division does not exist from Euclid's point of view; because Euclid regards parallel straight lines as never meeting and so the construction fails in this case.

Hence from Euclid's point of view it is impossible to state generally that to every point C on AB between A and B there corresponds a point C' such that C' divides AB externally in the same ratio as C divides AB, because there is no point corresponding to the middle point of AB.

From the point of view of Modern Geometry in which a straight line is supposed to have *one* point at infinity, when C is at the middle point of AB, C' is at infinity; and the theorem can be stated quite generally that there is one way of dividing AB internally and one way of dividing it externally in *any* given ratio $K : L$.

Art. 180.   NOTE 8.   On Art. 91.

The contents of Art. 91 may perhaps be more easily appreciated by considering the following numerical case.

Consider the triangle whose sides are a, b, c; and the triangle whose sides are $\dfrac{k^2}{a}, \dfrac{k^2}{b}, \dfrac{k^2}{c}$.

Then
$$b : c = \frac{k^2}{c} : \frac{k^2}{b};$$

$$c : a = \frac{k^2}{a} : \frac{k^2}{c};$$

$$a : b = \frac{k^2}{b} : \frac{k^2}{a};$$

so that any two sides of one triangle are proportional to some two sides of the other.

But the two triangles do not satisfy the condition in the enunciation of Prop. 29 implied in the words "taken in order."

E.g. whilst b corresponds to $\dfrac{k^2}{c}$ in the 1st proportion,

it corresponds to $\dfrac{k^2}{a}$ in the 3rd proportion.

As a numerical example take $a = 5$, $b = 3$, $c = 4$ and $k^2 = 60$.

Then $\dfrac{k^2}{a} = 12$, $\dfrac{k^2}{b} = 20$, $\dfrac{k^2}{c} = 15$;

and we have
$$3 : 4 = 15 : 20$$
$$4 : 5 = 12 : 15$$
$$3 : 5 = 12 : 20.$$

But since
$$5^2 = 3^2 + 4^2,$$
but
$$(20)^2 \neq (12)^2 + (15)^2;$$

the first triangle is right-angled, the second is not; and therefore the triangles are not similar.

Art. 181.   NOTE 9.   On Prop. 37.

In order to complete the proof of Prop. 37 without using Prop. 14 it is necessary to show directly that

if
$$A : B = T : U,$$
if
$$B : C = U : V,$$
and if $rA = sC$, then $rT = sV$.

If
$$rA = sC,$$
then
$$rA : B = sC : B.$$
Since
$$A : B = T : U,$$
$$\therefore rA : B = rT : U.$$ [Prop. 63.
Since
$$B : C = U : V,$$
$$\therefore B : sC = U : sV.$$ [Prop. 63.
$$\therefore sC : B = sV : U.$$ [Prop. 21.
$$\therefore rT : U = sV : U.$$
$$\therefore rT = sV.$$

$\therefore$ if $rA = sC$, then $rT = sV$.

Art. 182.   NOTE 10.   On Prop. 43.

The areas of similar triangles are proportional to the areas of the squares described on corresponding sides.*

Let *ABC, DEF* be similar triangles.

Let *AB, DE* be corresponding sides.

On *AB, DE* describe the squares *ABLK, DENM*.

It is required to prove that

$$\triangle ABC : \triangle DEF = \text{square } ABLK : \text{square } DENM.$$

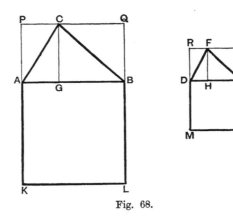

Fig. 68.

Draw *CG* perpendicular to *AB*, and *FH* perpendicular to *DE*.

Describe on *AB* the rectangle *ABQP* having the same altitude as the triangle *ABC*, and on *DE* the rectangle *DESR* having the same altitude as the triangle *DEF*.

The triangles *ACG, DFH* are similar, for

$$C\hat{A}G = F\hat{D}H,$$

$$C\hat{G}A = F\hat{H}D,$$

$$\therefore A\hat{C}G = D\hat{F}H.$$

---

* On account of the importance of this proposition an independent proof is given.

Hence the triangles are similar by Prop. 28.

$$\therefore CG : CA = FH : FD,$$

$$\therefore CG : FH = CA : FD, \qquad \text{[Prop. 24.}$$

but

$$CA : FD = AB : DE,$$

since the triangles are similar;

$$\therefore CG : FH = AB : DE,$$

i.e.

$$AP : DR = AK : DM,$$

$$\therefore AP : AK = DR : DM, \qquad \text{[Prop. 24.}$$

$$\therefore \text{rect. } ABQP : \text{square } ABLK = \text{rect. } DESR : \text{square } DENM,$$

$$\therefore \text{rect. } ABQP : \text{rect. } DESR = \text{square } ABLK : \text{square } DENM.$$

[Prop. 24.

Now

$$\text{rect. } ABQP = 2\triangle ABC$$

and

$$\text{rect. } DESR = 2\triangle DEF,$$

$$\therefore \text{rect. } ABQP : \text{rect. } DESR = \triangle ABC : \triangle DEF, \qquad \text{[Prop. 15.}$$

$$\therefore \triangle ABC : \triangle DEF = \text{square } ABLK : \text{square } DENM.$$

Art. 183.   NOTE 11.   On Prop. 57.

(α) In order to complete the proof of Prop. 57 without using Prop. 14 it is necessary to prove directly that

if

$$A : B = U : V,$$

if

$$B : C = T : U,$$

and if $rA = sC$, then $rT = sV$.

If

$$rA = sC,$$

then

$$rA : B = sC : B \ldots\ldots\ldots\ldots(\text{I}).$$

Now

$$A : B = U : V,$$

$$\therefore rA : B = rU : V \ldots\ldots\ldots(\text{II}). \qquad \text{[Prop. 63.}$$

Further

$$B : C = T : U,$$

$$\therefore C : B = U : T, \qquad \text{[Prop. 21.}$$

$$\therefore sC : B = sU : T \ldots\ldots\ldots(\text{III}). \qquad \text{[Prop. 63.}$$

From (I), (II), (III) it follows that

$$rU : V = sU : T \ldots\ldots\ldots(\text{IV}).$$

In the last result it is possible to transform the terms of the ratios so that the first term is the same in each.

$$rU : V = srU : sV \ldots\ldots\ldots(\text{V}), \qquad \text{[Prop. 15.}$$

$$sU : T = rsU : rT \ldots\ldots\ldots(\text{VI}). \qquad \text{[Prop. 15.}$$

From (IV), (V), (VI) it follows that

$$srU : sV = rsU : rT.$$

But $$srU = rsU,$$

$$\therefore \ sV = rT.$$ [Prop. 23.

$\therefore$ if $rA = sC$, then $rT = sV$.

(β) Propositions 37 and 57 are so nearly alike in form that the difference between them should be carefully noted.

Arranging them in parallel columns :—

	Prop. 37.		**Prop. 57.**
If	$A : B = T : U,$	If	$A : B = U : V,$
and if	$B : C = U : V,$	and if	$B : C = T : U,$
then	$A : C = T : V.$	then	$A : C = T : V,$

it appears that the positions of the ratios $T : U$, $U : V$ in Prop. 37 are interchanged in Prop. 57.

Art. 184.   NOTE 12.   ON PROP. 59.

The statement on lines 18 and 19 of Page 117 *that two ratios in which the first term is zero may be considered to be the same* may present some difficulty, inasmuch as a ratio presupposes the existence of two magnitudes, and the ratio of zero to a magnitude has not been defined.

Without going fully into the subject, which here touches upon the difficulties of the Infinitesimal Calculus, it may be sufficient to remark that since

$$\frac{A}{n} : A = A : nA,$$ [Prop. 15.

and $$\because \ A : nA = \frac{1}{n},$$

$$\therefore \ \frac{A}{n} : A = \frac{1}{n}.$$

Now imagine the integer n to increase without limit, then $\frac{A}{n}$ tends to the limit zero, and therefore the ratio $\frac{A}{n} : A$ is one in which the first term tends to the limit zero, whilst at the same time the ratio, viz. $\frac{1}{n}$, tends to the limit zero.

In this connection the following proposition is of interest.

If the ratio of A to B is the same as that of C to D; if A can be made as small as we please, and if B and D be fixed magnitudes, then C can be made smaller than any magnitude E, however small E may be.

It is possible by Archimedes' Axiom to choose n so that

$$nE > D;$$

and by hypothesis A can be taken smaller than $\dfrac{B}{n}$,

i.e.
$$nA < B,$$

$$\therefore \ A : B < \frac{1}{n}.$$

But
$$A : B = C : D,$$

$$\therefore \ C : D < \frac{1}{n},$$

$$\therefore \ nC < D,$$

$$\therefore \ nC < nE,$$

$$\therefore \ C < E.$$

So that when the first term of the ratio of A to B tends to zero, so also does the first term of the ratio of C to D.

Another proposition of a similar kind is this :—

If the ratio of A to B is the same as that of C to D; if A can be made as small as we please, if C and D be fixed magnitudes, then B can be made smaller than any magnitude E, however small E may be.

It is possible by Archimedes' Axiom to choose n so that

$$nC > D.$$

$$\therefore \ C : D > \frac{1}{n}.$$

Then since
$$A : B = C : D,$$

$$\therefore \ A : B > \frac{1}{n},$$

$$\therefore \ nA > B.$$

Now by hypothesis A can be made as small as we please.

Choose therefore

$$A < \frac{E}{n},$$

i.e. $$nA < E.$$

$$\therefore \; B < E.$$

Hence if the ratio of A to B be given, and one term tend to zero, so does the other.

Art. 185.   NOTE 13.   THE COMPOUNDING OF RATIOS.

The 37th Proposition is a very important one.

It is as follows :

if $$A : B = T : U,$$

and $$B : C = U : V,$$

then $$A : C = T : V.$$

Euclid describes the connection of the ratio $A : C$ with the ratios $A : B$ and $B : C$ by saying that the first ratio is compounded of the other two.

He uses the result in connection with Prop. 40, in which the ratio of the areas of two equiangular parallelograms is determined.

This terminology has not been employed in the text, because it is found difficult by beginners. On the other hand the object of the terminology, so far as the determination of the ratio of the areas of two equiangular parallelograms is concerned, is completely attained by the mode in which Prop. 40 is proved.

But the value of the terminology extends beyond its use in this proposition.

It will therefore be considered more at length.

Art. 186.   The development of the process of compounding ratios is made in four stages.

STAGE 1.   When it is necessary to determine the relative magnitude of two magnitudes, A and C, of the same kind, it is often convenient not to make the comparison directly, but indirectly by taking another magnitude B of the same kind as A and C; and then comparing A with B, and afterwards B with C.

From this point of view the relative magnitude of A and C is considered to be determined by the relative magnitude of A and B and the relative magnitude of B and C.

STAGE 2. Euclid expresses the general idea stated in the first stage by saying that the ratio of A to C is compounded of the ratio of A to B and the ratio of B to C.

STAGE 3. *Def.* 19. THE PROCESS OF COMPOUNDING RATIOS.

Let the ratios to be compounded be $P:Q$ and $T:U$.

Take any arbitrary magnitude A, and then find B so that

$$P:Q=A:B \quad \dots\dots\dots\dots\dots\dots\dots\dots\text{(I)},$$

and then find C so that $$T:U=B:C \dots\dots\dots\dots\dots\dots\dots\dots\text{(II)}.$$

Then the ratio compounded of $P:Q$ and $T:U$ is the ratio compounded of $A:B$ and $B:C$, and is therefore $A:C$ by the statement in the second stage.

This process* contains an arbitrary element, viz. A.

STAGE 4. In order to justify the process described in the preceding stage, it is necessary to show that the presence of the arbitrary element in the third stage has no influence on the value of the resulting ratio.

Suppose that instead of A, the magnitude A' had been selected, and that B' and C' had then been found so that

$$P:Q=A':B' \dots\dots\dots\dots\dots\dots\dots\text{(III)},$$

$$T:U=B':C' \dots\dots\dots\dots\dots\dots\dots\text{(IV)}.$$

Then the resulting ratio would be that compounded of $A':B'$ and $B':C'$, and would therefore be $A':C'$.

In order that this may agree with the previous result, it is necessary to show that

$$A:C=A':C' \quad \dots\dots\dots\dots\dots\dots\dots\text{(V)}.$$

From (I) and (III)

$$A:B=A':B' \quad \dots\dots\dots\dots\dots\dots\dots\text{(VI)}.$$

From (II) and (IV)

$$B:C=B':C' \dots\dots\dots\dots\dots\dots \dots\dots\text{(VII)}.$$

From (VI) and (VII) by Prop. 37, the proportion (V) follows.

Hence the process in the third stage always leads to the same value of the resulting ratio, whatever be the value of the arbitrary element.

This is the justification of the process described in the third stage.

* It should be noted that this process assumes the existence of B and C, when A has been chosen arbitrarily, the proof of which depends on the Fundamental Proposition in the Theory of Ratios (Art. 215).

Art. 187. ARITHMETICAL APPLICATION OF THE PROCESS FOR COMPOUNDING RATIOS.

To compound the ratio $r : s$ with the ratio $u : v$ where r, s, u, v are positive integers.

$$\left. \begin{array}{l} r : s = ru : su \\ u : v = su : sv \end{array} \right\} \text{ by Prop. 15.}$$

Hence $\qquad r : s$ compounded with $u : v$

$= ru : su$ compounded with $su : sv$

$= ru : sv$

by the definition of the ratio compounded of other ratios in Art. 186, Stage 2.

Now $\qquad\qquad\qquad \left. \begin{array}{l} r : s = \dfrac{r}{s}\,; \\[2ex] u : v = \dfrac{u}{v}\,; \\[2ex] ru : sv = \dfrac{ru}{sv}\,. \end{array} \right\}$ $\qquad$ [Art. 31.

and

Observe further that $\dfrac{ru}{sv}$ is defined to be the Arithmetical Product of $\dfrac{r}{s}$ and $\dfrac{u}{v}$, the result being written

$$\frac{r}{s} \times \frac{u}{v} = \frac{ru}{sv}.$$

Hence this arithmetical theorem corresponds to the theorem that

$$r : s \text{ compounded with } u : v = ru : sv.$$

Art. 188. *Def.* 20. DUPLICATE RATIO.

If a ratio be compounded with itself the resulting ratio is called the duplicate ratio of the original ratio.

Thus if $A : B$ be compounded with $A : B$, the resulting ratio is called the duplicate ratio of $A : B$.

Art. 189. PROPOSITION LXVII.

ENUNCIATION. *If three magnitudes be in proportion the first has to the third the duplicate ratio of the first to the second.*

Let $$A : B = B : C.$$

Then if $A : B$ be compounded with $A : B$, the result is the same as if $A : B$ be compounded with $B : C$, and is therefore $A : C$.   [Art. 186, Stage 2.

Hence $A : C$ is the duplicate ratio of $A : B$, if $A : B = B : C$.

Art. 190. PROPOSITION LXVIII.

ENUNCIATION. *If two ratios be equal, their duplicate ratios are also equal.*

If $$A : B = C : D \ \dots\dots\dots\dots\dots\dots\dots\dots\dots\dots(1),$$

it is required to prove that the duplicate ratio of $A : B$ is equal to that of $C : D$.

Take E so that $$A : B = B : E \ \dots\dots\dots\dots\dots\dots\dots\dots\dots\dots(2),$$

and F so that $$C : D = D : F \ \dots\dots\dots\dots\dots\dots\dots\dots\dots\dots(3).$$

Then by (1), (2), (3) $$B : E = D : F \ \dots\dots\dots\dots\dots\dots\dots\dots\dots\dots(4).$$

Hence from (1) and (4) $A : E = C : F,$ [Prop. 37.

But by (2) $A : E$ is the duplicate ratio of $A : B$ [Prop. 67.

and by (3) $C : F$ is the duplicate ratio of $C : D$,   [Prop. 67.

$\therefore$ the duplicate ratio of $A : B$ is equal to the duplicate ratio of $C : D$.

Art. 191. EXAMPLES.

89. Using the symbol $\divideontimes$ as an abbreviation for the words "compounded with," prove that

(i) $(A : B) \divideontimes (C : D) = (C : D) \divideontimes (A : B).$

(ii) $[(A : B) \divideontimes (C : D)] \divideontimes (E : F)$
              $= (A : B) \divideontimes [(C : D) \divideontimes (E : F)].$

90. Prove that $(A : B) \divideontimes [(B : A) \divideontimes (C : D)] = C : D.$

Hence show how to find the ratio which must be compounded with $A : B$ to give the ratio $C : D$.

91. Prove that $[(A : B) \divideontimes (C : D)] \divideontimes (D : C) = (A : B).$

92. If
$$E : C = A : P,$$
$$E : D = B : Q,$$
prove that
$$(A : B) \divideontimes (C : D) = (P : Q).$$

93. What is the result of compounding any ratio with a ratio of equality?

What is the result of compounding a ratio of equality with any ratio?

94. If a ratio be compounded with its reciprocal show that the result is a ratio of equality.

95. If A, B, C, D be magnitudes all of the same kind, prove that
$$A : B \text{ compounded with } C : D$$
gives the same result as
$$A : D \text{ compounded with } C : B.$$

96. Prove that $A : B$ compounded with $C : D$ gives $L : B$ where $D : C = A : L$.

97. If A, B, C, D are all magnitudes of the same kind, and
$$D : A \text{ compounded with } D : B$$
is equal to $D : C$, find the relation between A, B, C, D.

If A, B, C, D are all magnitudes of the same kind, and if $A : D$ compounded with $B : D$ give $C : D$, find the relation between A, B, C, D.

98. (i) What ratio must be compounded with $A : C$ to give $B : C$?

(ii) What ratio must be compounded with $C : A$ to give $C : B$?

99. If the duplicate ratio of $A : B$ be equal to the duplicate ratio of $C : D$, then prove that $A : B = C : D$.

100. (i) Prove the theorem of Menelaus; viz. if a straight line $A'B'C'$ cut the sides of the triangle ABC, viz. BC in A', CA in B', AB in C'; then the ratio compounded of the ratios
$$BA' : A'C, \quad CB' : B'A, \quad AC' : C'B$$
is a ratio of equality.

(ii) Prove the converse of the theorem of Menelaus: if the sides of the triangle $A'B'C'$ be divided, BC in A', CA in B', AB in C', so that two of the points of division are internal and one external, or else all three are external; and if further the ratio compounded of
$$BA' : A'C, \quad CB' : B'A, \quad AC' : C'B$$
is a ratio of equality, then the points A', B', C' lie on one straight line.

101. Prove that the six centres of similitude* of three circles lie three by three on four straight lines (called the axes of similitude of the circles).

[Apply the last example, taking A, B, C at the centres of the circles.]

* See Ex. 37, p. 73.

102. (i) Prove the theorem of Ceva, viz. :

If O be a point in the plane of the triangle ABC, if AO cut BC at A', if BO cut CA at B', if CO cut AB at C', then the ratio compounded of $BA' : A'C$, $CB' : B'A$, $AC' : C'B$ is a ratio of equality.

(ii) Prove the converse of the theorem of Ceva, viz. :

If the sides of the triangle ABC be divided, BC at A', CA at B', AB at C', so that two of the points of division are external and one internal, or else all three are internal, and if further the ratio compounded of $BA' : A'C$, $CB' : B'A$, $AC' : C'B$ is a ratio of equality, then the three straight lines AA', BB', CC' are concurrent.

Art. 192. *Def.* 21. CROSS OR ANHARMONIC RATIO.

If A, B, C, D be four points on a straight line, they determine six segments on that line.

Take any one of these six segments, say BD.

Then A divides it in the ratio $AB : AD$; and C divides it in the ratio $CB : CD$.

Then the ratio which must be compounded with either of these ratios to produce the other is *a* value of the cross or anharmonic ratio of the four points*.

Art. 193. EXAMPLES.

103. If A, B, C, D be four points on a straight line, and O any point not on that straight line, and if through B a straight line be drawn parallel to OD to cut OA at E and OC at F, then prove that

$$(CB : CD) \divideontimes (BE : BF) = (AB : AD).$$

104. By means of the preceding example prove that if four fixed straight lines passing through a point be cut by *any* fifth straight line, then the cross-ratio of the four points of intersection is independent of the position of the fifth straight line.

105. (i) If A, B, C are three points arranged in this order on a straight line L; if A', B', C' are any three points arranged in this order on another straight line L'; if the points A, B, C be joined to any point O; then prove that it is possible to draw a transversal $A''B''C''$ across the lines OA, OB, OC such that

$$A''B'' = A'B', \quad B''C'' = B'C'.$$

---

* This definition is sufficient for solving the problems set in this book. It is not however a complete one as the signs of the segments have not been specified. When the signs are specified, it can be shown that there are six values of the cross-ratio, all of which are determined when any one is given. One of these six values is $(AB : AD) \divideontimes (CD : CB)$ and is usually written $\dfrac{AB}{AD} \cdot \dfrac{CD}{CB}$.

(ii)   If through a point O any four straight lines be drawn, and these be cut by any transversal at A, B, C, D; if the straight lines joining any point O_1 to A, B, C, D be cut by any transversal at A_1, B_1, C_1, D_1; if the straight lines joining any point O_2 to A_1, B_1, C_1, D_1 be cut by any transversal at A_2, B_2, C_2, D_2; and if this process be repeated any number of times, so that four points A_n, B_n, C_n, D_n are finally obtained; then prove that it is possible to draw a transversal $A'B'C'D'$ across OA, OB, OC, OD such that

$$A'B' = A_n B_n, \quad B'C' = B_n C_n, \quad C'D' = C_n D_n.$$

(This is the geometric property which is unaltered by projection and corresponds to the constancy of the anharmonic ratio of four points on a straight line.)

106.   If A_1, B_1, C_1 be any three points on a straight line; and A_2, B_2, C_2 any three points on another straight line, show how to determine points D_1, D_2 on the two straight lines so that the cross-ratio of A_1, B_1, C_1, D_1 shall be equal to that of A_2, B_2, C_2, D_2. [On the straight line $A_1 A_2$ take any two points O_1, O_2. Let $O_1 B_1$, $O_2 B_2$ meet at B; let $O_1 C_1$, $O_2 C_2$ meet at C; then show that the points D_1, D_2 are such that $O_1 D$ $O_2 D_2$ intersect on BC.]

107.   If ABC be a triangle, if D be the middle point of BC, if any straight line through D cut AB at E, AC at F, and a parallel through A to BC at G, then find the value of the cross-ratio of E, D, F, G.

108.   If A, B, C, D be four fixed points on a circle, and P, Q any two other points on the same circle, prove that the cross-ratio of the four straight lines PA, PB, PC, PD is equal to that of the four straight lines QA, QB, QC, QD; and also to that of the four points in which the tangent at P to the circle is cut by the tangents at A, B, C, D.

109.   Let the points P, P' on the straight line OX be said to correspond when the rectangle $OP \cdot OP'$ is equal to a given rectangle. Then prove that the cross-ratio of any four points is equal to the cross-ratio of their corresponding points.

110.   If from any point two tangents be drawn to a circle, the points of contact and the points of intersection of any secant from the same point are such that the straight lines joining them to any fifth point on the circle form a harmonic pencil.

111.   (i)   Through any point O a tangent OU and a secant ORS are drawn to a circle; OPQ is another secant passing through the centre of the circle (P, Q being the extremities of a diameter). Show that if QR, QU, QS cut the tangent at P at R', U', S', respectively, then

$$PR' : PU' = PU' : PS'.$$

(ii)   If the point O be inside the circle, and U be taken as the extremity of the shortest chord through O, and the rest of the construction be as above, show that

$$PR' : PU' = PU' : PS'.$$

Art. 194.   NOTE 14.   THE AGGREGATING OF RATIOS.

On proposition 62 depends the process, called in this book the Aggregating of Ratios, which corresponds to the addition of the measures of the ratios.

The development of this process is made in four stages.

STAGE 1. The general idea at the root of the process of aggregating ratios is this :—

When it is desired to find the ratio of one magnitude to a second, it is permissible to break up the first magnitude into two parts, then to find the ratio of each part to the second magnitude, and then to add the two ratios thus found.

(It should be carefully noticed that it is the first magnitude, *not the second*, which may be broken up.)

STAGE 2. To make the general idea stated in the first stage quite precise the following definition is necessary.

Let the ratio $X + Y : Z$ be said to be aggregated from the ratios $X : Z$ and $Y : Z$. It is known when the magnitudes X, Y, Z are known.

(This may be compared with Euclid's 22nd Datum.)

Let the symbol $\frown$ placed between two ratios denote that they are to be aggregated.

Then
$$X + Y : Z = (X : Z) \frown (Y : Z).$$

STAGE 3. In the second stage the two ratios which are aggregated both have the same second term, and therefore do not at first sight appear to be entirely independent.

It is necessary therefore to explain what is meant by aggregating *any* two ratios, i.e. two ratios whose terms are all independent.

Def. 22.   THE PROCESS OF AGGREGATING RATIOS.

Let the ratios to be aggregated be $A : B$ and $C : D$.

Take any arbitrary magnitude Z.

Then find* two others X and Y such that
$$A : B = X : Z,$$
$$C : D = Y : Z.$$

---

* This assumes the Fundamental Proposition in the Theory of Ratios (Art. 215).

Then $\qquad (A:B) \frown (C:D)$

$$= (X:Z) \frown (Y:Z)$$
$$= X + Y : Z.$$

STAGE 4. The *form* of the resulting ratio found in the third stage depends on the value of the arbitrary magnitude Z. If the process is to be of any use it is necessary to show that the *value* of the resulting ratio does not depend on the *value* of Z.

This will be accomplished when it is shown that if any other magnitude be taken, say Z', instead of Z, and the process repeated, then the value of the resulting ratio is unaltered.

Let therefore X', Y' be found so that

$$A:B = X':Z',$$
$$C:D = Y':Z'.$$

Then $\qquad (A:B) \frown (C:D)$

$$= (X':Z') \frown (Y':Z')$$
$$= X' + Y' : Z'.$$

Since $\qquad A:B = X \; : Z,$

and $\qquad A:B = X':Z',$

$$\therefore \; X:Z = X':Z'.$$

Since $\qquad C:D = Y \; :Z,$

and $\qquad C:D = Y':Z',$

$$\therefore \; Y:Z = Y':Z'.$$

Since $\qquad X:Z = X':Z',$

and $\qquad Y:Z = Y':Z',$

$$\therefore \; X + Y : Z = X' + Y' : Z'. \qquad \text{[Prop. 62.}$$

i.e. the *value* of the resulting ratio is unaltered.

This is the justification of the process, and shows that it always leads to consistent results.

Art. 195.   EXAMPLES.

112.   Prove that

$$(A:B) \frown (C:D) = (C:D) \frown (A:B).$$

113.   Prove that

$$[(A:B) \frown (C:D)] \frown (E:F)$$
$$= (A:B) \frown [(C:D) \frown (E:F)].$$

Art. 196. ARITHMETICAL APPLICATION OF THE PROCESS OF AGGREGATING RATIOS.

If r, s, u, v are integers, prove that

$$(r : s) \frown (u : v) = (vr + us : vs).$$

$$\left[\text{This corresponds to the Arithmetical Theorem } \frac{r}{s} + \frac{u}{v} = \frac{vr + us}{vs} . \right]$$

Now $r : s = vr : vs$ [Prop. 15.

and $u : v = us : vs.$ [Prop. 15.

$$\therefore (r : s) \frown (u : v)$$

$$= (vr : vs) \frown (us : vs)$$

$$= vr + us : vs.$$

Art. 197. EXAMPLE 114.

Prove that $[(A : B) \frown (C : D)] \divideontimes (E : F)$

$$= [(A : B) \divideontimes (E : F)] \frown [(C : D) \divideontimes (E : F)].$$

Art. 198. NOTE 15. INTRODUCTION OF THE IRRATIONAL NUMBER INTO ANALYSIS*.

There are two direct operations which can always be performed on integers, viz. addition and multiplication; and the results are always positive integers.

If however an attempt is made to reverse these processes, the result is not always a positive integer, e.g. if any two positive integers a and b being given, it is desired to find the number, which when added to a will give b, the result will be a positive integer only when b is greater than a.

Again if it is desired to find the number which when multiplied by a will give b, the result will be a positive integer only when b is an integral multiple of a.

In order that it may be always possible to reverse the process of addition it is necessary to invent the negative integer, and in order that it may be always possible to reverse the process of multiplication, it is necessary to invent the positive rational fraction.

* The ideas on which this note is based are due to Dedekind, as stated in the Preface.

If two positive rational fractions are added together, the result is always a positive rational fraction; but if it is desired to reverse the process of addition of positive rational fractions, it is necessary to invent the negative rational fraction.

The positive integers, the negative integers, the positive rational fractions and the negative rational fractions, are together said to form the system of rational numbers, and the system may be denoted by the letter R.

Art. 199.   If $\dfrac{p}{q}, \dfrac{r}{s}$ be any two rational numbers, then it is known that

$$\frac{p}{q} = \frac{ps}{qs},$$

$$\frac{r}{s} = \frac{qr}{qs}.$$

There are now three possibilities.

$$(1) \quad ps > qr,$$

$$(2) \quad ps = qr,$$

$$(3) \quad ps < qr.$$

In case $\qquad\qquad (1) \quad \dfrac{ps}{qs} > \dfrac{qr}{qs},$

$$\therefore \frac{p}{q} > \frac{r}{s}.$$

In case $\qquad\qquad (2) \quad \dfrac{ps}{qs} = \dfrac{qr}{qs},$

$$\therefore \frac{p}{q} = \frac{r}{s}.$$

In case $\qquad\qquad (3) \quad \dfrac{ps}{qs} < \dfrac{qr}{qs},$

$$\therefore \frac{p}{q} < \frac{r}{s}.$$

In case (2), $\dfrac{p}{q}$ and $\dfrac{r}{s}$ are not regarded as essentially distinct.

Art. 200.   The first property of rational fractions to be proved is that

if $\qquad\qquad\qquad\qquad \dfrac{p}{q} > \dfrac{r}{s},$

and if $\qquad\qquad\qquad\qquad \dfrac{r}{s} > \dfrac{t}{u},$

then $\dfrac{p}{q} > \dfrac{t}{u}.$

Since $\dfrac{p}{q} > \dfrac{r}{s},$

                                            $\therefore\ ps > qr.$ (I)

Since $\dfrac{r}{s} > \dfrac{t}{u},$

                                            $\therefore\ ur > ts.$ (II)

$\therefore$ by (II) $pur > pts,$

                                            $\therefore\ pur > t\,(ps).$ (III)

Now from (I) $t\,(ps) > t\,(qr).$ (IV)

Hence from (III) and (IV) $pur > tqr,$

                                            $\therefore\ pu > tq.$

                                            $\therefore\ \dfrac{p}{q} > \dfrac{t}{u}.$

Art. 201. A geometrical analogy to this proposition is as follows :—

If A, B, C be three points on a straight line, and if A be to the right of B and if B be to the right of C, then A is to the right of C.

Art. 202. The second property of the system of rational numbers to be proved is that between any two distinct rational numbers, another rational number always exists.

Let $\dfrac{p}{q}$ and $\dfrac{r}{s}$ be two distinct rational numbers, then the rational number $\dfrac{ps + rq}{2qs}$ lies between them.

Suppose $\dfrac{p}{q} > \dfrac{r}{s},$

                                            $\therefore\ ps > qr.$

It is to be proved that

$$\dfrac{p}{q} > \dfrac{ps + rq}{2qs} > \dfrac{r}{s}.$$

To prove $\dfrac{p}{q} > \dfrac{ps + rq}{2qs}$, it is necessary to show

$$2ps > ps + rq,$$
$$ps > rq,$$

which is the case.

To prove $\dfrac{ps + rq}{2qs} > \dfrac{r}{s}$, it is necessary to show

$$ps + rq > 2rq,$$
$$\therefore \ ps > rq,$$

which is the case.

Art. 203. A geometrical analogy to the above result is as follows:—

If A and B be any two distinct points on a straight line, then another point C lies between them.

Art. 204. Now let $\dfrac{r}{s}$ be any positive rational number. Then all the numbers belonging to the system of rational numbers, viz. R may be separated into two groups or classes as follows.

Into the first class, which may be called the lower class and which may be denoted by R_1, let there be put all the positive rational numbers less than $\dfrac{r}{s}$, and all the negative rational numbers.

Into the second class, which may be called the upper class, and which may be denoted by R_2, let there be put all the rational numbers greater than $\dfrac{r}{s}$.

Let $\dfrac{r}{s}$ be put into either class, it does not matter which.

If $\dfrac{r}{s}$ be put into R_1, it is the greatest number in R_1.

If $\dfrac{r}{s}$ be put into R_2, it is the least number in R_2.

In either case the separation of the system of all the rational numbers R into the two classes R_1, R_2 is such that every number of the lower class R_1 is less than every number of the upper class R_2.

Art. 205. The following is a geometrical analogy to the preceding.

If P be a point in any straight line then all the points in the straight line may be separated into two classes P_1, P_2, as follows.

The first class, P_1, contains all the points that lie on one side, say the left, of P.

The second class, P_2, contains all the points that lie on the right of P.

The point P itself may be put into either class, it does not matter which.

If P be put into the class P_1, then the class P_1 has a point, viz. P, which is the farthest to the right, but the class P_2 has no point which is farthest to the left.

If P be put into the class P_2, then the class P_2 has a point, viz. P, which is the farthest to the left, but the class P_1 has no point which is farthest to the right.

In either case the separation of all the points on the straight line into the two classes P_1, P_2 is of such a nature that every point of the first class P_1 is on the left of every point of the second class P_2.

Art. 206. It will now be shown that it is possible to separate the system of *all* the rational numbers R into two classes such that

(*a*) every number in one class (the lower class) is less than every number in the upper class;

(*b*) the lower class has no greatest number;

(*c*) the upper class has no least number.

Note carefully the distinction between this enunciation and that of the separation of the system of rational numbers effected by means of $\dfrac{r}{s}$, in which either the lower class had a greatest number, or the upper class had a least number.

Art. 207. *Algebraic illustration of the separation of the system of rational numbers into two classes possessing the characteristics* (*a*), (*b*) *and* (*c*) *of* Art. 206.

Let D be a rational number, which is not the square of any rational number.

Let all positive rational numbers whose squares are greater than D be placed in the upper class.

Let all positive rational numbers whose squares are less than D, and all negative rational numbers, be placed in the lower class.

It will be proved that the upper class has no least number, and that the lower class has no greatest number.

Let x be any rational number.

Let
$$y = \frac{x^3 + 3xD}{3x^2 + D} \quad\dotfill(\text{I}).$$

Then, since x and D are rational, it follows that y is also rational.

From (I) it follows that

$$y - x = \frac{2x(D - x^2)}{3x^2 + D} \quad\dotfill(\text{II}),$$

and

$$y^2 - D = \frac{(x^2 - D)^3}{(3x^2 + D)^2} \quad\dotfill(\text{III}).$$

Now choose any number x in the upper class, so that

$$x^2 > D,$$

then $\qquad\qquad\qquad\qquad$ $y < x$, by (II),

and $\qquad\qquad\qquad\qquad$ $y^2 > D$, by (III).

Hence y is in the upper class, but is less than x.

Hence the upper class has no least number.

Next let x be in the lower class

$$\therefore\ x^2 < D,$$

$$\therefore\ y > x,\ \text{by (II)},$$

and $\qquad\qquad\qquad\qquad$ $y^2 < D$, by (III).

Hence y is in the lower class, but is greater than x.

Hence the lower class has no greatest number.

The numbers in the lower class are all less than the numbers in the upper class.

Since no rational fraction exists whose square is equal to D, it follows that all the rational fractions have been separated into two classes, which possess the characteristics (a), (b), (c) of Art. 206.

Art. 208. *Geometric illustration of the separation of the whole system of rational numbers into two classes, possessing the characteristics (a), (b), (c) of Art.* 206.

Let A and B be two segments of straight lines, which have *no* common measure.

Let $\dfrac{n}{r}$ be any rational fraction.

Let Q be a magnitude such that $B = rQ$.

Now let the magnitude nQ be compared with A.

Then A cannot be equal to nQ, for then Q would be a common measure of A and B, which is assumed not to be the case.

Hence either $A < nQ$, or $A > nQ$.

If $\qquad\qquad\qquad\qquad$ $A < nQ$,

then $\qquad\qquad\qquad\qquad$ $A : B < nQ : B$, $\qquad\qquad$ [Art. 43.

$$\therefore\ A : B < nQ : rQ.$$

$$\therefore\ A : B < \frac{n}{r}.$$

This being so, let $\dfrac{n}{r}$ be assigned to the upper class.

But if $A > nQ,$

then $A : B > nQ : B,$

$\therefore\ A : B > nQ : rQ,$

$\therefore\ A : B > \dfrac{n}{r}.$

In this case let $\dfrac{n}{r}$ be assigned to the lower class.

Hence every rational fraction falls into one of the two classes.

Those in the upper class are greater than $A : B$.

Those in the lower class are less than $A : B$.

Hence every rational fraction in the lower class is less than every rational fraction in the upper class.

Art. 209.   It will next be proved

(i) *that the lower class contains no greatest number.*

(ii) *that the upper class contains no least number.*

(i)   Let $\dfrac{n}{r}$ be any rational number in the lower class.

Choose Q so that $B = rQ$.

Then by the preceding argument $A > nQ$.

Since A is not a multiple of Q, it must lie between two consecutive multiples of Q.

Let $sQ < A < (s+1)\,Q$.

Now n cannot be greater than s, for sQ is the greatest multiple of Q which is less than A.

If n be less than s, then since

$$B = rQ, \quad A > sQ.$$

Therefore $\dfrac{s}{r}$ is a rational number in the lower class, which is greater than $\dfrac{n}{r}$.

If however $n = s$, then

$$A - sQ < Q.$$

Choose t so that

$$t\,(A - sQ) > Q.$$

Let V be a magnitude such that
$$Q = tV,$$
$$\therefore \; t\,(A - stV) > tV,$$
$$\therefore \; A - stV > V,$$
$$\therefore \; A > (st + 1)\,V \, ;$$
but
$$B = rQ = rtV,$$
$$\therefore \; A : B > (st + 1)\,V : rtV,$$
$$\therefore \; A : B > \frac{st + 1}{rt},$$
$$\therefore \; \frac{st + 1}{rt} \text{ is in the lower class} ;$$
but
$$\frac{st + 1}{rt} > \frac{st}{rt},$$
$$\therefore \; \frac{st + 1}{rt} > \frac{s}{r},$$
$$\therefore \; \frac{st + 1}{rt} > \frac{n}{r}.$$

Hence in each case a rational number greater than $\frac{n}{r}$ exists which is in the lower class.

Hence the lower class has no greatest number.

(ii)   Let $\frac{n}{r}$ be any rational number in the upper class.

Then if
$$B = rQ,$$
$$A < nQ.$$

As before let
$$sQ < A < (s + 1)\,Q.$$

Then n cannot be less than $(s + 1)$.

If
$$n > s + 1.$$

Then
$$\frac{s + 1}{r} < \frac{n}{r},$$

and
$$\frac{s + 1}{r} \text{ is in the upper class.}$$

But if
$$n = (s + 1),$$
then since
$$(s + 1)\,Q - A \text{ is less than } Q,$$

find t so that

$$t\left[(s+1)\,Q - A\right] > Q.$$

As before let

$$Q = tV,$$

$$\therefore \; t\left[(s+1)\,tV - A\right] > tV,$$

$$(s+1)\,tV - A > V,$$

$$A < \left[(s+1)\,t - 1\right]V.$$

Now

$$B = rQ = rtV,$$

$$\therefore \; A : B < \left[(s+1)\,t - 1\right]V : rtV,$$

$$\therefore \; A : B < \frac{(s+1)\,t - 1}{rt}.$$

Hence

$$\frac{(s+1)\,t - 1}{rt} \text{ is in the upper class.}$$

Now

$$\frac{(s+1)\,t - 1}{rt} < \frac{(s+1)\,t}{rt},$$

$$\therefore \; \frac{(s+1)\,t - 1}{rt} < \frac{s+1}{r},$$

$$\therefore \; \frac{(s+1)\,t - 1}{rt} < \frac{n}{r}.$$

Hence a rational number smaller than $\dfrac{n}{r}$ has been found, which is in the upper class.

Hence the upper class has no least number; and the lower class has no greatest number. Also every number in the lower class is less than every number in the upper class.

Hence the existence of the two incommensurable magnitudes A, B renders it possible to separate the whole system of rational numbers into two classes possessing the characteristics, marked (a), (b), (c) in Art. 206.

Art. 210. *Correspondence between the rational numbers and the points on a straight line.*

If we select any origin O on the line, and a unit of length, then to the rational number $\dfrac{r}{s}$ there will correspond a point P whose distance from O is equal to $\dfrac{r}{s}$ units of length, and which is on a definite side of O, previously chosen. In the same way, the negative rational numbers will correspond to points on the line on the other side of O.

Thus all the positive and negative rational numbers correspond to definite points on the straight line.   But it is not true conversely that all the points on the straight line correspond to rational numbers.   For example, if the side of a square be taken as the unit of measurement, and a length OP be measured from the origin on the line equal to the diagonal of the square, then to the point P on the line no rational number will correspond, because as has been shown (Note 5, Art. 177), the side and diagonal of a square are incommensurable.

Now it may be proved that there are an infinitely great number of lengths, which are incommensurable with the unit of length.

Therefore the straight line has an infinite number of points which do not correspond to the rational numbers.

If therefore it is desired to construct a number which shall correspond to each point on a straight line, then it is clear that the system of rational numbers will not suffice, and it is therefore necessary to invent new numbers, so that the system of numbers invented shall possess the same degree of completeness as the straight line.   This property of completeness is called the continuity of the straight line.

The preceding comparison of the system of rational numbers R with the points on a straight line has led to the recognition of the fact that whilst all rational numbers correspond to points on a straight line, all points on a straight line do not correspond to rational numbers.

Consequently there exist gaps in the system of rational numbers; there is an incompleteness or discontinuity in this system; whilst the straight line is considered to be free from gaps and to possess completeness or continuity.

It is necessary to explain in what this continuity consists.

It was shown in Art. 205 that every point P of a straight line separates the straight line into two parts such that every point of one part lies to the left of every point of the other part.

The essence of continuity consists in the converse of the above, viz. in the following principle.

" If all points of the straight line fall into two classes such that every point of the first class lies to the left of every point of the second class, then there exists one and only one point which produces this separation of all points of the straight line into two classes."

This principle is known as the Cantor-Dedekind Axiom.   It cannot be proved. It is the Axiom by means of which we attribute continuity to the straight line.

Compare this with the following statement regarding the system of rational numbers.

EUCLID, BOOKS V. AND VI.

" If all rational numbers are separated into two classes such that every number of the first class is less than every number of the second class, *then only when the first class has a greatest number or the second class a least number* does there exist a rational number which produces this separation of all the rational numbers into two classes."

We can now proceed to complete the discontinuous system of rational numbers so as to obtain therefrom a continuous system.

Just as negative and fractional numbers are invented and introduced into analysis, and as the laws of operating with these numbers may be reduced to the laws of operating with positive integers, so it is necessary to invent irrational numbers and to define them by means of the rational numbers alone.

It appears from the preceding discussion that if any rule be given for separating all rational numbers into two classes such that every number in the lower class is less than every number in the upper class, the following are the possible alternatives :—

(i) the lower class has a greatest number and the upper class has no least number ;

(ii) the upper class has a least number and the lower class has no greatest number ;

(iii) the lower class has no greatest number and the upper class has no least number.

Suppose that in case (i) the greatest number in the lower class is $\frac{r}{s}$.

If this number $\frac{r}{s}$ is transferred to the upper class, there will be formed another separation of all the rational numbers into two classes such that every number in the lower class is less than every number in the upper class, but this separation of the system of rational numbers is regarded as essentially the same as the one from which it was produced by the transfer of $\frac{r}{s}$ from the lower to the upper class.

Both separations are regarded as produced by $\frac{r}{s}$; and $\frac{r}{s}$ is the number which corresponds to the separation.

In case (iii) the separation is not produced by any rational number. It is regarded as produced by an irrational number, which is said to correspond to the separation.

Dedekind called a separation a 'cut.' It will be called here a 'section.'

It is in this property that all sections of the system of rational numbers cannot be produced by rational numbers that the incompleteness or discontinuity of the system of rational numbers consists.

An irrational number is regarded as known, whenever a rule is given for determining whether any given rational number belongs to the lower or upper class of the section of the system of rational numbers to which the irrational number corresponds because all the properties of the irrational number can be deduced from a knowledge of the numbers contained in these two classes.

It is usual to denote the irrational number itself by a single symbol.

Hence to every section of the system of rational numbers there corresponds a definite rational or irrational number.

For example, the irrational number corresponding to the section described in Arts. 208 and 209 is equal to the ratio of A to B.

Two numbers are regarded as different or unequal only when they correspond to *essentially* different sections.

The aggregate of all the rational and irrational positive and negative numbers is called the aggregate of *real* numbers.

Art. 211.   *Operations with real numbers.*

To reduce any operation with two real numbers α, β to operations with rational numbers, it is necessary to show how from the section (A_1, A_2), which defines α, and the section (B_1, B_2) which defines β, to define another section (C_1, C_2) which is to correspond to the result of the operation.

As examples consider the cases of addition and multiplication of two irrational numbers α, β.

*Let p_1 be any number in A_1,
              p_2 .... A_2,
              q_1 .... B_1,
              q_2 .... B_2.

It will be proved that by a suitable choice of these numbers it is possible to make

$$(p_2 + q_2) - (p_1 + q_1),$$

and $$p_2 q_2 - p_1 q_1,$$

as small as we please.

Write down in order of magnitude the rational fractions whose denominator is n.

There must be some stage at which we pass from the lower to the upper class of α.

* In this and some of the following articles small letters *with suffixes* denote rational fractions.

Let

$$\frac{m}{n} < a < \frac{m+1}{n}.$$

Divide the interval $\left(\dfrac{m}{n}, \dfrac{m+1}{n}\right)$ into t equal parts, and consider the fractions whose denominators are tn, viz.

$$\frac{tm}{tn}, \frac{tm+1}{tn}, \ldots\ldots \frac{tm+t}{tn}.$$

The first belongs to the lower class of a, the last belongs to the upper class of a.

Hence an integer k exists, such that

$$\frac{tm+k}{tn} < a < \frac{tm+k+1}{tn}. \qquad (k+1 \gtreqless t)$$

In like manner we can find

$$\frac{r}{n} < \beta < \frac{r+1}{n},$$

$$\frac{rt+l}{tn} < \beta < \frac{rt+l+1}{tn}. \qquad (l+1 \gtreqless t)$$

Take now

$$p_1 = \frac{tm+k}{tn}, \quad p_2 = \frac{tm+k+1}{tn},$$

$$q_1 = \frac{rt+l}{tn}, \quad q_2 = \frac{rt+l+1}{tn},$$

$$\therefore (p_2 + q_2) - (p_1 + q_1) = \frac{2}{tn},$$

$$p_2 q_2 - p_1 q_1 = \frac{tm + tr + k + l + 1}{t^2 n^2}.$$

Now

$$k < t,$$

$$l + 1 \gtreqless t,$$

$$\therefore k + l + 1 < 2t,$$

$$\therefore p_2 q_2 - p_1 q_1 < \frac{m + r + 2}{n^2} \cdot \frac{1}{t}.$$

Now suppose m, r, n to be fixed; then by increasing t without limit, it follows that $(p_2 + q_2) - (p_1 + q_1)$ and $p_2 q_2 - p_1 q_1$ can each be made as small as we please.

Art. 212. Now consider the case of *addition*.

Form all possible sums of the form $p_2 + q_2$, and put every rational number which is greater or equal to any sum of this form into a class, which may be called the upper class.

Form all possible sums of the form $p_1 + q_1$, and put every rational number which is less or equal to any sum of this form into another class, which may be called the lower class.

Let s_1 be a number of the lower class.

Let s_2 be a number of the upper class.

Then it is always possible to find p_1, p_2, q_1, q_2 such that

$$s_1 \lesseqgtr p_1 + q_1,$$
$$s_2 \gtreqless p_2 + q_2.$$

But
$$p_1 < p_2, \quad q_1 < q_2,$$
$$\therefore \ s_1 < s_2.$$

Hence every number in the lower class is less than every number in the upper class.

It will next be shown that the two classes include all the rational numbers with the possible exception of *one* rational number.

If possible let there be two distinct rational numbers a, b which belong to neither class.

If a do not belong to the upper class, a is less than every sum of the form $p_2 + q_2$.

If a do not belong to the lower class, a is greater than every sum of the form $p_1 + q_1$.

Hence if a belong to neither class $p_1 + q_1 < a < p_2 + q_2$.

Similarly
$$p_1 + q_1 < b < p_2 + q_2,$$
$$\therefore \ (p_2 + q_2) - (p_1 + q_1) > a \sim b.$$

But it has been shown that $(p_2 + q_2) - (p_1 + q_1)$ can be made as small as we please. Hence it can be made smaller than $a \sim b$, which is contrary to what has been proved.

Hence two distinct rational numbers, each of them belonging to neither class, cannot exist.

It is therefore proved that there can exist at most one rational number which belongs to neither class, but it is not proved that there is one such rational number.

Consequently there may be no rational number which belongs to neither class.

If one rational number exist which does not belong to either class, it is greater than all the numbers in the lower class and less than all the numbers in the upper class. Put it into either class, and a section will be defined by the two classes so formed. The number corresponding to this section is the single rational number just mentioned, and it is called the sum of α and β.

If no rational number exist, which does not belong to either class, then all the rational numbers belong to either the lower or upper class. Hence the two classes define a section. The number corresponding to this section is an irrational number. This irrational number is defined to be the sum of α and β.

Art. 213. Next consider the case of *multiplication*.

Now the upper class consists of all the rational numbers which are greater or equal to any product of the form $p_2 q_2$.

The lower class consists of all the rational numbers which are less or equal to any product of the form $p_1 q_1$.

The demonstration may be obtained from the demonstration in the case of addition by replacing throughout the word 'sum' by the word 'product', $p_1 + q_1$ by $p_1 q_1$, and $p_2 + q_2$ by $p_2 q_2$.

Art. 214. *On the Compounding of Ratios.*

Let the ratio of A to B be equal to α.

Let the ratio of B to C be equal to β.

Let p_1^*, p_2 be rational numbers in the lower and upper class of α.

Let q_1, q_2 be rational numbers in the lower and upper class of β.

Then
$$p_1 B < A < p_2 B,$$
$$q_1 C < B < q_2 C,$$
$$\therefore \ p_1 q_1 C < p_1 B$$
$$< A$$
$$< p_2 B$$
$$< p_2 q_2 C,$$
$$\therefore \ p_1 q_1 C < A < p_2 q_2 C.$$

---

* If $p_1 = \dfrac{s}{r}$, and $A : B > p_1$,

then $A : B > \dfrac{s}{r}$,

                                                        $\therefore \ rA > sB$,

                                                        $\therefore \ A > \dfrac{sB}{r}$.

This is also written $A > \dfrac{s}{r} B$.

If therefore $A : B > p_1$, then $A > p_1 B$.

Hence if the ratio of A to C be equal to γ, then every p_2q_2 and all greater numbers are in the upper class of γ, whilst every p_1q_1 and all smaller numbers are in the lower class of γ.

Consequently $\qquad\qquad \gamma = \alpha\beta$, by Art. 213.

Hence if $\qquad\qquad A : B = \alpha$, and if $B : C = \beta$,

then $\qquad\qquad\qquad A : C = \alpha\beta$.

Art. 215. PROPOSITION LXIX.

(The Fundamental Proposition in the Theory of Ratio.)

ENUNCIATION. *If A, B be two magnitudes of the same kind, and if C be any third magnitude, to prove that there exists a fourth magnitude Z, such that*

$$A : B = C : Z.$$

It is sufficient to prove that there exists a magnitude Z such that $Z : C = B : A$.

(1) If B and A be commensurable, let

$$B : A = \frac{r}{s}.$$

Then it is necessary to find Z, so that

$$Z : C = \frac{r}{s}.$$

Form the magnitude $\qquad\qquad \dfrac{rC}{s}.$

Then $\qquad\qquad \dfrac{rC}{s} : C = s\left(\dfrac{rC}{s}\right) : sC$ $\qquad\qquad$ [Prop. 15.

$$= rC : sC$$

$$= \frac{r}{s}.$$

Hence $\qquad\qquad Z = \dfrac{rC}{s}.$

(2) If B and A have no common measure, let $B : A$ be equal to the irrational number ρ.

Let $p_1, p_1', p_1'', \ldots$ represent rational numbers in the lower class of ρ in ascending order of magnitude.

Let $p_2, p_2', p_2'', \ldots$ represent rational numbers in the upper class of ρ in descending order of magnitude.

Let the magnitudes

$$p_1C, \quad p_1'C, \quad p_1''C, \quad \ldots,$$
$$p_2C, \quad p_2'C, \quad p_2''C, \quad \ldots$$

be constructed.

Then $\qquad p_1C < p_1'C < p_1''C < \ldots < p_2''C < p_2'C < p_2C.$

Consider now the set of all the magnitudes of the same kind as C. They fall into two classes.

(i) Those which are greater than every magnitude of the form p_1C. Call any magnitude of this form a magnitude Y.

(ii) Those which are not greater than every magnitude of the form p_1C. Call any magnitude of this form a magnitude X.

In the first place it will be proved *that every magnitude Y is greater than every magnitude X.*

From the definition of the magnitudes X, it appears that any X, say X_1, does not exceed every magnitude of the form p_1C.

Suppose that X_1 does not exceed the magnitude $p_1'C$.

Then by the definition of the magnitudes Y, every Y exceeds every p_1C and therefore every Y exceeds $p_1'C$.

But X_1 does not exceed $p_1'C$.

Therefore Y exceeds X_1.

Therefore every Y exceeds every X.

In the second place it will be shown *that the set of magnitudes X include no greatest magnitude.*

The characteristic of the magnitudes X is that they are not greater than every magnitude p_1C.

Suppose X' one of the magnitudes X, and let $X' \gtreqless p_1'C$.

Now there is no greatest p_1.

Suppose $\qquad p_1' < p_1'',$

then $\qquad p_1'C < p_1''C.$

Take then $X'' = p_1''C$, which is possible.

$$\therefore \ X'' > X'$$

and so on other magnitudes X can be found in increasing order of magnitude.

Thus the magnitudes X include no greatest magnitude.

Now the magnitudes X and Y together include all the magnitudes of the same kind as C. In regard to these magnitudes we assume an axiom corresponding to the Cantor-Dedekind Axiom for the straight line, as follows:

"If all the magnitudes of the same kind as C be separated into two classes such that every magnitude of the one class is less than every magnitude of the other class, then there is one and only one magnitude of the same kind as C which produces this separation, and it is either the greatest magnitude of one class, or the least magnitude of the other class."

Now we have proved that the magnitudes X include no greatest magnitude.

Therefore the magnitudes Y include a least magnitude.

Call this least magnitude Z.

Since the magnitude Z is a magnitude Y, therefore Z is greater than every magnitude of the form $p_1 C$.

Write this thus:
$$Z > \text{every } p_1 C,$$
$$\therefore Z : C > \text{every } p_1.$$

We have next to prove that
$$Z : C < \text{every } p_2,$$
$$\textit{i.e. } Z < \text{every } p_2 C.$$

Suppose if possible
$$Z \geqq \text{some } p_2 C.$$

Then since the rational numbers p_2 include no least rational number, let
$$p_2 > p_2'.$$

Form the magnitude $p_2' C$.

Then
$$p_2' C < p_2 C,$$
$$\therefore p_2' C < Z.$$

Now
$$\text{every } p_2 > \text{every } p_1,$$
$$\therefore p_2' > \text{every } p_1,$$
$$\therefore p_2' C > \text{every } p_1 C,$$

therefore $p_2' C$ is a magnitude Y.

But
$$p_2' C < Z.$$

Hence there is a magnitude Y, which is less than Z; which is contrary to the definition of Z, viz. that it was the least of the magnitudes Y.

Hence
$$Z < \text{every } p_2 C,$$
$$\therefore Z : C < \text{every } p_2.$$

And it was proved that
$$Z : C > \text{every } p_1.$$

Hence $Z : C$ determines the same section as the irrational number ρ, $\textit{i.e.}$ the same section as $B : A$.
$$\therefore B : A = Z : C,$$
$$\therefore A : B = C : Z.$$

INDEX

The references are to the Articles.

For EU product safety concerns, contact us at Calle de José Abascal, 56–1°,
28003 Madrid, Spain or eugpsr@cambridge.org.

www.ingramcontent.com/pod-product-compliance
Ingram Content Group UK Ltd.
Pitfield, Milton Keynes, MK11 3LW, UK
UKHW030902150625
459647UK00021B/2675